# Praise for *Dial Up*

"*Dial Up the Dream* helps mothers understand how best to support their daughters as they move from adolescence to adulthood. Each chapter is full of relatable stories, practical advice, and exercises to help moms bring the best version of themselves to their mother-daughter relationship. Breathe slower and deeper as Colleen O'Grady walks you through the steps to parent your daughter from a place of love—not fear—and, in the process, develop a closer and more meaningful connection."

**JEANNINE JANNOT**, PhD, author of *The Disintegrating Student: Struggling but Smart, Falling Apart, and How to Turn It Around*

"Colleen O'Grady is the best kind of author, teacher, and therapist. The kind who has not only mastered the research and science, but has also been in the trenches of parenthood herself. In *Dial Up the Dream*, Colleen navigates the complexity and hardship of letting go of your freedom-obsessed daughter while expertly guiding you to rediscover your own life. A must-read for any mom who is ready to open her heart and rediscover her truth."

**CHRISTINE KANE**, author of *The Soul-Sourced Entrepreneur: An Unconventional Success Plan for the Highly Creative, Secretly Sensitive & Wildly Ambitious*

"As mothers, we dream of being close with our grown daughters. We instinctively know that how we handle their teenage and young adult years sets the stage for this lifelong relationship—and whether we become a source of comfort or stress for them. In *Dial Up the Dream*, Colleen O'Grady offers a compassionate, empowering, and relevant guide to help moms of young adults become the friend, mentor, and cheerleader they need. This book offers powerful insight on how to help your daughter thrive after she leaves home and also step into the role of being her biggest fan. I highly recommend it."

**KARI KAMPAKIS**, mom of four girls; author of *Love Her Well: 10 Ways to Find Joy and Connection with Your Teenage Daughter*; host of the *Girl Mom Podcast*

"This is a must-read for all parents on how to navigate the intense relationship that exists between mothers and daughters and how to tap into the potential of healthy and powerful connections that will last a lifetime. Colleen O'Grady has nailed what it takes to truly connect with your daughter during difficult times and how to triumph in the parenting relationship to ensure your daughter has a happy, independent life."

NEHA GUPTA, founder, College Shortcuts

"This wonderful book touches the heart of the mother-daughter relationship during the journey to adulthood. It captures—beautifully and practically—the difficult task of separating, letting go, and, at the same time, remaining close. Such a gift to the world."

EINAT NATHAN, parenting expert; author of *My Everything: The Parent I Want to Be, the Children I Hope to Raise*

"*Dial Up the Dream* is a roadmap for moms who want the best for their daughters as they move from teen to adult. This book is full of practical tools to empower mom to best support her daughter to dial up her dream while maintaining a healthy relationship with her. Mom can rest knowing her daughter can tap into her truth and find a college and career that is authentic to her."

DR. AVIVA LEGATT, PCC, founder, Ivy Insight; author of *Get Real and Get In: How to Get Into the College of Your Dreams by Being Your Authentic Self*

"*Dial Up the Dream* is a must-read for mothers with adolescent daughters who are entering emerging adulthood. Through stories, analogies, and practical exercises, Colleen O'Grady explains the brain science behind your child's behavior, and provides evidence-based strategies for navigating your relationship with your daughter as she transitions to independence. But even more than that, this book is about navigating your relationship with yourself and the 'what next?' phase that comes with launching your daughter from your home into the world."

DANIELLE M. DICK, PhD, distinguished Commonwealth professor; author of *The Child Code: Understanding Your Child's Unique Nature for Happier, More Effective Parenting*

# DIAL UP
## THE
# DREAM

# DIAL UP

## THE
## DREAM

Make Your Daughter's
Journey to Adulthood the Best—
*For Both of You*

**COLLEEN O'GRADY**

••
**PAGE TWO**

Some names and identifying details have
been changed to protect the privacy of individuals.

This book is not intended as a substitute for the medical advice
of physicians. The reader should regularly consult a physician
or psychiatrist in matters relating to his/her/their health
and particularly with respect to any symptoms that may require
diagnosis or medical attention.

Cataloguing in publication information is available
from Library and Archives Canada.
ISBN 978-1-77458-145-2 (paperback)
ISBN 978-1-77458-146-9 (ebook)
ISBN 978-1-77458-147-6 (audiobook)

Page Two
pagetwo.com

Edited by Emily Schultz
Copyedited by Rachel Ironstone
Proofread by Alison Strobel
Cover and interior design by Taysia Louie
Printed and bound in Canada by Friesens
Distributed in Canada by Raincoast Books
Distributed in the US and
internationally by Macmillan


22 23 24 25 26   5 4 3 2 1


colleenogrady.com

*I dedicate this book to every authentic, imperfect,
and invested mom who desires an ongoing and gratifying
relationship with her daughter as she journeys to
adulthood. Not only is mom committed to her daughter's
dreams, she wonders what's possible for her.
On her good days she knows there's a dream for her too!*

# Contents

# Introduction

TOLD MY twenty-five-year-old daughter I was headed to La Jolla, California, to write the introduction to this book. "Can I come?" she asked. I was dubious at first. At home in Houston, it only takes one dirty window to distract me from writing. Having her in my sightline—my favorite person in the world, the best of all possible distractions—no way would I get any work done. So, of course, I said yes. And no, I didn't do any writing for the two days she was with me. I had to extend my trip to finish this introduction. And yes, the delay was absolutely worth it.

During our time together, we watched the seals in La Jolla Cove as we drank our morning coffee. We found fun places to eat, hike, and lie on the beach. She got a mani, I got a pedi. We poked around art galleries. She "needed" to buy sunglasses, and we both bought earrings. Last night, as we watched the sun set over the Pacific, she took a selfie of us with the sun shining through one of her new hoop earrings.

Through it all, we talked and talked. In this relaxed space, she told me about all the good things in her life—her business expanding and her committed relationship—and she shared her struggles too. This time and these conversations are precious to me now that she lives in another city. Also, because it wasn't always like this.

She left this morning at 5 a.m. to catch a plane home and return to her adult world. Her boyfriend is picking her up from the airport. These goodbyes are never easy, though I know I'll probably see her in a couple of months. During these mini reunions, I'm on top of the world. Such visits are the premier jackpot of dopamine hits for a mom. But visits are temporary. And it stings every time I say goodbye. As she nears twenty-six, our relationship is such a blessing to me. She continues to get me out of my routine, inspire me, and teach me how to have fun.

## From Drama to Dream

If you'd told me eight years ago as my daughter was entering her senior year in high school that I would a) have full confidence in her making a predawn flight on her own; b) feel at peace with her ability to make big life decisions, not to mention run a business; and c) be sad when she left but also kind of excited to get back to my life—well, I would have wondered if you'd ever met me.

Now, as I look out over La Jolla Cove all by myself and settle in to write, I think about all the twists and turns I and every mom experience as our daughters slowly make the move from living under our roofs and by our rules to independence and figuring out their own rules as they inch toward their dreams. I think about how in the last eight years my relationship with my daughter has changed, grown, and matured as she walked (sometimes stumbled) toward adulthood—and as I walked (often stumbling) toward becoming the mother of an adult woman.

As a marriage and family therapist with a private practice specializing in the mother-daughter relationship, I've spent the last twenty-eight years helping moms and their teen-to-young-adult daughters positively navigate the murky waters of these transformative years.

My last book, *Dial Down the Drama*, provides moms with the insights and strategies needed to successfully manage their daughters' early-to-mid-teens, while keeping their relationship strong. This book, *Dial Up the Dream*, focuses on the stage of development from the late teens through the mid-twenties—when your daughter takes flight and begins to build her own life. In some ways, this emerging-adult stage can be more stressful on both mother and daughter than the teen years because the stakes are higher and the changes to the relationship more profound.

Of course, each stage of parenting has its unique trials and difficulties. What makes the emerging-adult stage exceptional, though, is how unprepared most of us moms are for it. We all know to brace ourselves for the turbulent teens. And when we're up to our necks in our teen's drama, we cling to the belief that when she finally leaves home, the hard part of parenting will be done. Even better, our mother-daughter relationship will be good again.

That's not how it works.

The drama and rash decision-making don't miraculously disappear at high school graduation. They dissipate… slowly… over the next several years as her brain develops toward full maturity, which typically occurs around the age of twenty-five. Yet at eighteen, she'll be regarded by the law as an adult. While her brain is still forming, she'll likely move out of your house, live independently for the first time, and make career and relationship decisions that could impact the rest of her life.

If you feel your mommy-dar going off about now, I get it. As you look at your eighteen-year-old daughter today—overemotional, naive, and shockingly impulsive—you rightly wonder if she's up to the task of separating her laundry properly, let alone keeping herself alive. Though you love her and believe wholeheartedly in the person she's becoming, you honestly question the wisdom of allowing her to live anywhere or make any decisions without adult supervision at this point in her development.

Adding to the tension is that your world is changing too. As she gains her independence, you're losing a job that's defined you for nearly two decades, a job you love. While she gets ceremonies and congratulations to mark each milestone, there's no accompanying ritual or even acknowledgment for the changes in your life. After talking with a mom about her nineteen-year-old daughter, she messaged me this:

*As a mom, you're just supposed to keep smiling as you wave goodbye. Of course, I want my daughter to be independent and have a life she loves. But at the same time, her leaving has left me with an ache in my heart and a hole in my life that I'm not sure what to do with. Sometimes I get so sad not seeing her every day (even though half the time she lived here, I was mad at her). But there's no space for mourning, and no one to talk to about it. Especially if your child is doing well, you feel like a self-absorbed jerk for being sad. I always wondered if any other moms felt like this, or if I was just crazy.*

Rest assured, a lot of other moms feel this way—I see them all the time in my practice. Also rest assured, your role as "mom" is not coming to an end. It's simply changing. Your daughter still needs you. And since you're the only one in the relationship with the fully formed brain at the moment (not to mention life experience), it's up to you to see both you and your daughter successfully through this phase in her life, while keeping your relationship strong. How to do that; what you need to know and understand; and the strategies, tools, and practices you need to put in place are all found in these pages.

## This Way to the Dream: What's in This Book

*Dial Up the Dream* is the book my clients have been requesting for years; it's the book *Dial Down the Drama* readers have been asking for now that their daughters are graduating from high school; and it's the book I wish someone had given me when my daughter was taking those first steps toward independence.

This book validates what you are feeling and experiencing with your daughter right now. Beginning with her late high school years and moving stage by stage to her young adulthood, it lets you know what to expect next, how to manage it, and how to be there for her in the most supportive and helpful ways, whatever comes. In these twelve chapters, you learn

* exactly what's going on with her emotionally and physiologically, and how to use this science-based knowledge to set realistic expectations, reduce tensions, and not take her behavior personally;

* how to think about and navigate the many complex feelings in this journey for both you and your daughter;

* how to get the most from your daughter's last years at home and create a home she wants to visit once she moves away;

* the most common emotional traps we moms get caught in during these years and how to avoid them;

* why it's imperative to change your parenting role from monitor to trusted consultant—and how to do that;

* how to judge when your intervention in her life is called for and when to let her find her own way;

* what to do and what not to do when your daughter suffers a major setback... and why she probably will;

* why you must recognize and heal your own mothering trauma— and how to do that;

* how to use this new phase in your daughter's life to dial up your own dreams—and why doing so is imperative to your daughter's development and to a having a vibrant, meaningful, lifelong mother-daughter relationship.

Each chapter ends with an exercise so you can put what you learn into practice immediately.

## The Dream Is Within Your Reach Now

After nearly two decades together, the emotions and identities of mothers and daughters often become entangled like a drawer full of old necklaces. Through what you find in this book, you can free yourself and your daughter from those parts of your relationship that snag you and keep you stuck. You can move into this next stage in your mother-daughter relationship having smoothed out the knots between you and shining side by side, as two adults, each in your unique way.

This emerging-adult phase can be confusing, confounding, and even painful at times. But it is also an amazing time of personal growth for your daughter and for you. When you approach it with an understanding of what's happening and why, knowledge of how to manage it, and a fully open heart, this time of transition lays the foundation for her dreams—and yours—and for a relationship you both will cherish forever.

Mom, I know you are more than up to the challenge!

# 1

# The Junior-Senior Parenting Zone

JEN HAD just come from work, wearing a white jacket, black skinny jeans, and red pumps. Her makeup looked fresh. Her long hair had soft curls that were impressively still in place at 6 p.m. Just beneath that perfect exterior, however, I sensed exhaustion as she walked through my office door.

"How can I help you?" I asked.

"I'm miserable," Jen said, before she even hit the couch. "My daughter Emily is a senior in high school. I don't know if I'll survive the year. She's being a total hornet. Every time I bring up something about her college applications or her college essays, she pushes back with a rapid, 'I know, I know, I know.' Obviously, she doesn't 'know,' because her grades are dropping, and she keeps procrastinating. Everything with her is a huge battle. She's either in her room with the door shut, or she's out with her friends. When she does talk to me, she's just mean."

We both took a breath.

If you're struggling with your junior- or senior-high-school-aged daughter, you're not alone and you're not imagining the trials ahead. In this stage of her growth and your parenting, there are so many challenges, obstacles, stressors, and traps for the mother-daughter relationship. But there are also so many opportunities to revel in the person she's becoming and to be there for her as she takes her next step to claiming her own life and dreams.

I know because I've lived it with my own daughter, who's now twenty-five. I've also spent more than fifty thousand hours as a licensed marriage and family therapist and coach helping moms and daughters navigate this perplexing passage.

What I shared with Jen in my office that day, and what I'm sharing here with you, is that from those late teen years and into their mid-twenties, our daughters can be unwise, immature, and unrealistic—and yes, overly dramatic about everything. But what I've found in my practice and through my personal experience is that we as mothers sometimes make things worse even when we think we're being helpful.

But that doesn't have to be. By becoming more self-aware and by better understanding where your daughter is developmentally through each phase of her walk to adulthood, you can make things better for her and for you. With a little knowledge and the right tools, you can learn how not to react to the drama but instead to act from a place of belief in her and the desire to support her as she does the difficult work of maturing. As she slowly makes the transition from teenage girl to adult woman, you can ensure she has the space she needs to develop the self-confidence and life skills to eventually take full responsibility for herself. And you can do it all the while keeping the bond between you strong.

Where Jen, and maybe you, are right now—that last year in high school and at home—most of the drama between mother and daughter is caused by our laser-focus on our daughter's future. It's hard to be present in a relationship when your mind and mouth are always running six months ahead. But by focusing on the here and now, and by using this last year or so at home to prepare our daughters for the independence that's just around the corner, we can be responsible parents and at the same time enjoy our kids. We can ensure our daughters have what they need to launch into life, while also relishing the time we still have with them—allowing them to continue to brighten our lives with their energy, playfulness, and their anything-is-possible spirit.

Though your daughter is less dependent on you and spending most of her time with her friends, you're still important to her. Even though she acts like you're not. You are a stabilizing and comforting presence in her life—the voice of reason as she prepares to leave home. The truth is she needs you now more than ever.

## If Moms Could Go There Again...

When we're on the verge of milestone moments in life, we often have trouble distinguishing what's truly important and what just isn't. (Like bridezillas, we can overreact. Because we are fearful, we can be over-the-top controlling and critical. In other words, not fun to be around.) So I asked my community of moms, "What would you have done differently in your daughter's senior year in high school?" I loved their honest responses:

- "I'd educate myself better on how to respond during conflicts. I'd try harder to parent my teen without being so afraid. And I'd learn not to take things personally."

- "I wish I'd worked more on communication skills. I needed to really listen to her perspective and opinions instead of automatically saying no."

- "I'd focus more on connecting and less on correcting. I'd spend more time coaching, nudging, and supporting. I'd focus on her gifts and strengths, and not worry so much about the condition of her room."

- "I would not parent out of fear."

- "I think I'd be more appreciative of the transition she was in, that she really had one toe in high school and a foot in college. I should've listened to her."

- "If I could've done something differently in the past year, I would've celebrated our bond by doing more silly things together... things that would create memories that would stand out for both of us."

There's a lot of hard-earned wisdom to mine from these moms as you yourself move into this new phase of parenting. "I'd focus more on connecting and less on correcting" is at the heart of their advice. In other words, because they got caught up in all the drama, they missed opportunities for getting what they really wanted—an authentic, close, and even enjoyable relationship with their daughters in their last year at home.

If you're in the heat of the battle with your daughter, this may seem impossible from where you sit now. Don't lose heart. It's eminently doable. Here's where we begin...

## Start Your Transition

Let's play a little game. Let's say reality has hit. Your daughter is now a junior in high school.

Quick. What's your number one focus?

If you're thinking something like, "To make sure my daughter keeps her grades up so she can get into a good college," welcome to the Always-Stressed-and-Never-Rest Moms' Club.

Hey, it's not as if you didn't care about your daughter's grades in her sophomore year (and all through her schooling). But then you mostly left the day-in, day-out responsibilities of her studies to her— stepping in only when there was an issue.

All of a sudden, the moment you realize she's starting her junior year, the OMG-we-need-to-get-serious-*now* alarm goes off in your head. Your brain puts out an all-points bulletin that your daughter's future is at stake like never before. You panic. The pressure rides in. You think, *I need to double down*, which means you think your daughter needs to double down. Your eye is on the prize. Which for many moms, including you, means that your daughter graduates from high school and gets accepted into the right college. You have a future focus, an end goal. Low grades are the enemy. It feels like it's all on you to push this thing through.

And that's exactly how you don't get the most out of your daughter's last few years at home—for either of you.

I have spent my career listening to moms tell me what matters to them. Here's what I know: Everything you do for your daughter, you do to help her attain her dreams. You want her to be successful and happy. So, every time you confront her for failing a test or her lack of motivation; every time you march into her room and say, "Stop FaceTiming your boyfriend and study for your SAT"; every time you push her to work on her college essay; every single time you tell her what to do or what not to do—you do it for her sake. For her future.

Here, I invite you to take a step back and ask yourself what the consequences of your incessant "reminding" are. For all your effort, does your daughter say, "Mom, I really appreciate you. I know I've been edgy and mean to you, but thank you so much for being such a good mom. I'm going to do as you say"?

I seriously doubt it. She probably lashes out at you or avoids you. And for all your effort, are you accomplishing your goals? Do you feel she's inspired by your constant prodding to do her best? My guess is it probably feels like you can never get a break. Despite how hard you try, you feel ignored, ineffective, and misunderstood. You worry that you don't have the skills, the patience, or the energy to parent her through the challenges ahead.

So, let's acknowledge that you love your daughter, you're a great mom, and all your intentions are in the right place. But let's also acknowledge that your message is clearly not getting through—no matter how often or how loud you yell.

Why? Because you're obsessing, not connecting here. And you can't be heard if you can't connect. To have a healthy relationship with your daughter, she needs to be truly seen, and this won't happen when you're caught up in your agenda for her.

## Stop Obsessing: Nix the Powerless Parenting Message

So, what do you think it's going to be like between you and your daughter in these last two years or less at home? In other words, what are your expectations?

Are they positive? *I look forward to having more quality time with my daughter and watching her progress.*

Or negative? *I'm dreading this. It's going to be a huge battle. I am going to have to be on my daughter constantly.*

Maybe a little of both?

Most parents default to negative expectations when it comes to teenagers—mostly because we've been conditioned in that direction by our culture. We want to brace ourselves for the worst, be prepared for the battle, and hope nothing bad happens. All the while, we're battling fear—fear for their future and for our future without them—that only gets heightened as graduation day gets closer.

As a mom of an older teen daughter, your typical Powerless Parenting Message might go something like this: *The end goal, my daughter's future, is more important than my daughter's well-being and our relationship.* Supporting thoughts might include, *I'm not supposed to be my daughter's best friend.* Which is code for, *She can hate me. I don't care. I'm going to push her over the finish line come hell or high water. In fact, she is supposed to hate me because that's the only way she'll leave home.*

Our culture embeds such Powerless Parenting Messages in us. We may not even be aware of them—so we never question them. Yet, they drive how we think, feel, and parent.

Implied in these messages is that the end justifies the means. This is binary—either-or—thinking: either your daughter completes her lab report and hates you, or your daughter fails her lab and loves you. Your messaging is telling you that your choices (her success vs. a good relationship between you) are mutually exclusive—you can't have both. But this just isn't true.

When it comes to parenting—especially parenting an older teen— the end does not justify the means. Looking to attain some "end goal" for your teen with no care as to how you get her there, with no care as to how she feels, will only undermine her trust in you. It can damage her self-image, erode her confidence, and jeopardize your relationship.

Beyond making us irritable, harboring negative messaging disempowers us as parents. If all you're doing is fighting, then you're not tuned in to your daughter. You won't know how she feels, what she's thinking, or what's in her heart. If you're always on her back, you risk her hiding from you and not reaching out when the issue is more serious than an overdue term paper. Even if she does come to you, you won't be available for her emotionally.

These negative messages also rob us of our joy as parents and our ability to create positive experiences with our teens. They bring tension into our homes and affect our health. We end up missing out on all the good stuff, the simple, ordinary things, like playing with the dog together on your bed or talking in the kitchen. The things we'll miss the most once our daughters are in college. These also happen to be the times she's likely to relax and let you in.

Cultivating positive, empowering messaging around your mother-daughter relationship is essential for effective parenting and vital for your daughter's well-being—not to mention a more enjoyable way to spend her last few years at home. Moving into a positive mindset that encourages connection begins by pulling ourselves out of the traps that keep us stuck in an obsessing, negative mindset.

## Escape the College Trap

As their tweens become teens, I counsel parents to look out for three specific traps—I call them drama traps—common to this stage of parenting:

1 a fixed future focus
2 a fear drive always at full throttle
3 a need to control that's out of control

If parents don't learn to manage these traps in their teen's freshman or sophomore year, by junior and senior year, these parents tend to end up in one big drama trap that I call the College Trap.

As a parent, you know you're caught in the College Trap when you become obsessed about everything regarding your daughter's post-high school life. You want to control every aspect of it. If college is where she's headed, you monitor her grades, oversee her admissions essays, schedule campus visits, and so on. You're so fearful for her future that you become preoccupied with it, causing you to turn a blind eye—intentionally or unintentionally—toward how she's doing emotionally, physically, and socially right now. You no longer recognize—so you can no longer take advantage of—opportunities to connect with her.

When I asked Jen what exactly prompted Emily's reactions toward her, she replied with a story most moms in this phase of parenting can relate to: "Just about anything sets her off. Like when I tell her she needs to bring her grades up if she's going to get into a good college. Or when I remind her she needs to get her homework done and prepare for her SAT. Or when I tell her to return a call to an admissions counselor."

"How does that make you feel?" I asked.

"Emily frustrates me so much! She has so much going for her, but she's unmotivated and lazy." Jen sighed and got quiet. Then she added, "It's okay, I'm not supposed to be her best friend. I only have one year left of this."

Jen, like most moms, thought she was doing what she was supposed to be doing as a mother—securing Emily's future—even if it made them both miserable. That drive combined with her Powerless Parenting Message ("Emily is unmotivated and lazy" and "I'm not supposed to be her best friend") now had Jen stuck firmly in the College Trap. With all eyes on the future, Jen was looking right past her daughter, seriously limiting her ability to parent.

## The College Trap Prevents You from Connecting

The College Trap narrowed Jen's view to the tip of the iceberg of Emily's issues (not studying, not getting her college applications done). She didn't think to look for what was lurking underneath the surface.

If Jen could have broadened her focus, she would've seen that Emily was stuck in dramas of her own: Like she'd had a steady friend group up until this year when some misunderstanding split the group in two, creating a rift between Emily and her best friend. Then, piling drama upon drama as only teenage girls can, Emily desperately wanted a boyfriend, yet she was anxious around boys. The anxiety had caused her to drink too much at a party and get sick. She'd passed out in front of all her peers and now was humiliated—only adding to her preoccupation with what others were saying about her.

With all this and other typical teenage angst, Emily's confidence dropped, along with her grades. She started to feel stupid and worried about getting into college at all. Not to mention that underneath all the senior year excitement, she was a little apprehensive about graduating and leaving home.

This is why Emily was finding it hard to focus on homework and college applications—not because she was lazy or unmotivated. Sometimes she'd stare at her homework for hours and wouldn't remember anything. She felt like her mom didn't care about her; she only cared about her grades. She felt her mom was always mad at her.

None of Emily's issues was unusual or insurmountable. If Jen had been tuned in, she could have really helped Emily understand what was going on in her life, make some better choices, and move forward. Which was Jen's true goal all along—and what they both wanted.

As Jen and I worked on the College Trap in her sessions, she came to see how it kept her in her own story, closed her off from Emily, and made parenting an older teen nearly impossible. The next step was to set herself free.

That began by changing her Powerless Parenting Message into a Powerful Parenting Message. One that would empower Jen to create the relationship she wanted with her daughter, continue to be a responsible parent, and get the most out of this next year with Emily.

## Create a Powerful Parenting Message

A Powerful Parenting Message starts with a positive vision for what your relationship with your daughter can be.

Jen wanted to like Emily again and for Emily to like her. "Well, at least be able to be in the same room," she said. "I also want Emily to become more autonomous—but still feel she can turn to me when she needs to. Does that make sense?"

It did. I then encouraged Jen—and now I'm encouraging you: Think about who *you* would need to be to realize the relationship you've defined. What would that look like in real life? How do you and your daughter treat each other? What's the dynamic between you?

Then create a Powerful Parenting Message that expresses that.

If you're like most moms I see in my practice, your new Powerful Parenting Message might go something like this:

*I trust my daughter and support her in her best next step. I choose to listen to, enjoy, and stay connected with my daughter.*

It's one thing to say it, I know. But to make it your mindset means thinking through and understanding every phrase—not just what they mean intellectually, but what each will demand from you, and what living each will look like in your everyday interactions with your daughter. For instance, the first phrase in the message: "I trust my daughter." Trusting a teenager isn't easy. They're works in progress. And our comfortable old drama traps, fear and control, can creep up and blind us from seeing our teen's strengths, character, and abilities.

So, if this is part of your message, you might find the power to live this phrase by turning your attention toward what you *do* trust in your daughter. What are her strengths? What areas does she succeed in? What about resiliency? Where has she bounced back from a mistake? How has she gotten back on track? Where do you see her making an effort? What do teachers or other parents say about her? Is she creative? Is she innovative? Is she a leader? Why do her friends like her?

Consider that even her negative traits can point you toward her strengths. Is she strongheaded? Is she persistent? Will she push back? These can be positive traits too.

As you work through your message, I encourage you to journal. This is what turned things around with Jen. I challenged her to focus on Emily's positive traits. Then write down one thing she is grateful for, one area where she sees progress, and one thing she delights in. I asked her to do this every day for a week and see how that changed how she felt about Emily. It made a big difference. Jen came into our next session more relaxed. She even smiled for the first time.

So, on to the next phrase in the message: "… and support her in her best next step." You have to know what your daughter considers her "best next step" before you can support it. That requires you to know your daughter right now—not who she was at ten or who she wants to become or who you want her to become. If you don't know her, then you're only pushing for what you think is best (the right college or the right major). So, Mom, this part of the message requires you to be present and open-minded.

But be prepared. Her "best next step" might not be what you would choose for her. And that can be hard. However, consider that it just might be what's right for her. Jen thought she knew the "best next step" for Emily—college, of course. But during one of our sessions, Jen realized she'd never asked Emily what she wanted. I coached Jen to honestly ask Emily in a quiet and sincere way, and then listen, really listen.

So later that week, when Jen and Emily were both relaxed and driving back from Starbucks, Jen said, "Emily, I've pushed you so hard because I thought I knew what was best for you. But I want to know what you want."

Jen kept her demeanor calm, though inside she braced herself for Emily's answer. Bringing us—and Jen—to the last part of your Powerful Parenting Message: "I choose to listen to, enjoy, and stay connected with my daughter." This means that no matter what's going on in your world, you take time to check in with your daughter. You ask her about her day and then give her one hundred percent of your attention for the next five minutes. If during this time you find yourself obsessing about the condition of her room or if she's studied enough for the midterm, you need to put your monitoring hat aside and focus solely on the issues in her heart—like what is going on with her friends or who she's dating.

Be aware that sometimes your daughter bids for your attention by saying things like, "Mom, watch this YouTube video." She may not be ready to talk yet, but she wants to connect. When these moments pop up, put aside thoughts like, *This is a total waste of time.* Take advantage of her offer to enjoy (okay, maybe *endure* is a better word here) a few minutes watching something of interest to *her*. Often, as you share this experience together, she'll automatically open up.

Jen started practicing this with Emily. It was hard for her to take off her monitoring hat, but she thought, *Anything is possible for five or ten minutes.*

To Jen's surprise, within a week Emily started opening up to her. Even though Emily was closing in on eighteen, Jen realized that her daughter needed her. But (as we'd discussed in session) in different ways than Jen had thought. Emily needed her mom's love and reassurance. She needed a safe place to vent all her complicated emotions. She needed her mom's guidance. She needed a stable place to get grounded and de-stress.

To do all this for her daughter, which Jen desperately wanted to do, meant Jen needed to hear what Emily was saying—and not saying—as she answered that question in the car on the ride home from Starbucks.

"Yes, Mom, I want to go to college," Emily said in a rote tone. Then, she withdrew, waiting for Jen to pounce, to tell her that if that's what she wanted she better get her grades up and get her essays done.

But Jen didn't do that. To Emily's shock, Jen apologized. "I'm sorry I've been hard on you. I deserved that answer. But dear, I really do want to know how you are and what you want."

Emily, still defensive, said, "Mom, this has been a horrible year for me, and you don't even care!"

"I am so sorry, but I'm here now."

It took a few miles and about half a latte, but eventually Emily softened and poured out her life. It was hard for Jen to hear about how much Emily had struggled with her friends and that she passed out at a party, but she was grateful to know what was going on in her daughter's heart. They connected.

"Of course I want to go to college. I just feel so dumb compared to my friends," Emily confided. "They make perfect grades and don't even study."

Jen's instinct was to pounce, but she stayed true to her Powerful Parenting Message and held her tongue. She thoughtfully asked, "How badly do you want to go to college?"

"I don't want to be at home when all my friends are gone," Emily said. "I want it bad."

"How can I help?" Jen asked. "Would it be helpful if you had a tutor? I really want to help, even if it's just taking you through the drive-thru at Chick-fil-A." With this lighthearted gesture, Jen was letting Emily know she was willing to lay aside her agenda. And she knew Emily truly loved Chick-fil-A.

Emily laughed and gave her mom a big smile.

One of the most loving and productive things you can do as a parent is to let go of your agenda for twenty minutes and listen. Really, it's a privilege. She's letting you in. Only when you truly know what's in her heart and soul can you guide her well.

A Powerful Parenting Message doesn't eliminate the worries or the challenges—either yours or your daughter's. What it does do is give you a positive perspective from which to meet those challenges. It keeps you in the present and clear on your intentions. Most of all, it encourages you to connect with your daughter, so you can be there, and she can trust you to guide her toward being self-sufficient while making the most of her last years at home.

## Stepping Into Your Powerful Parenting Message

As with any major mindset shift, living your Powerful Parenting Message doesn't just happen presto! It's a two steps forward, one step back kind of proposition for most of us. However, by putting two things in place—a practice of self-awareness and a support team—before you start on this journey, you make it much easier to keep moving in the right direction.

Many outside forces are pulling on us all the time. As parents of older teens, we feel pressure to corral them to get on the "right path." Moms can feel this gavel of judgment over their heads, driving them like mother machines to keep pushing. But know, left unchecked, these forces eventually pull you right out of yourself and back into powerless messaging and drama traps.

A practice of self-awareness lessens the power of those outside forces and keeps your focus on what you truly want—your daughter's happiness. Even if we're pulled away from time to time, self-awareness can bring us back into alignment with our Powerful Parenting Message, so we stay connected to our teen.

Self-awareness takes the ability to distance yourself from you and your situation, like climbing up the bleachers of a stadium and looking down at the field of your life. This space allows you to observe and be curious in order to ask yourself orienting questions, like: What's really going on with my teen? What's going on with me? Why am I exhausted? Why am I so stressed? What am I really afraid of? Why am I not happy? Why do I not like my teen right now? Is this who I want to be in this moment? Does this thing I'm yelling about really matter? What do I need?

Self-awareness is not a critical, mean voice; it's a kind and compassionate voice that courageously addresses the truth. Self-awareness leads you to take responsibility for your life. It frees you from seething in negative emotions such as judgment, bitterness, and resentment. Self-awareness keeps you anchored to your humanness and your vulnerability, which allows you to see your daughter's humanness and vulnerability. You become aware of what you need.

The second thing that can be a real help in staying true to your Powerful Parenting Message is help—support from outside sources, like family, friends, neighbors, tutors, driving instructors, whatever and whomever can lighten your load. Because there's no need to carry this junior-senior angst all alone. And there's no reason you should be the go-to expert for everything your teen needs.

For your own emotional support, start out by finding one trusted person who you can be totally real with, especially when you have a lot whirling around in your brain. My daughter could get my head spinning her junior year. She had no shortage of ideas for after high school. She would say things like, "I want to go to school in London."

"I want to go to school in California." "I want to go to school in New York City." "I want to work at Starbucks in New York City and not go to school." And there were many more.

Each time she would tell me her new idea, I felt sheer panic. Then I'd calm down because I thought the moment had passed, and then there was her next new idea, and repeat, I'd be in panic mode again. These were the times I picked up my phone and called my sister. She was my trusted person and knew how to bring me back to center.

Your spouse, of course, seems like a natural choice for emotional support. Consider, though, that they might be just as freaked out about your child's choices and behaviors as you are. Also, often clients tell me that when they turn to their husbands for understanding, they instead get criticism and impatience. That's not what you need.

If you choose to reach out to your own mother, just be aware that you might find she doesn't understand because her parenting was so different from yours. I don't think my mom stressed about me getting into college for two seconds. It wasn't because my grade point average was amazing; actually, it was the opposite. I had a GPA that would make today's moms cringe. But it just wasn't hard getting into the state university then. I applied and was admitted.

You might seek out and talk to moms who have kids already in college. They have a perspective you need—mostly, they can tell you it's going to work itself out. And they can assure you that even though their teen didn't get into their dream college, their child ended up exactly where they needed to be.

Going to a psychotherapist or a life coach can be a huge gift to yourself at this time. It doesn't mean you're a failure; it means you want the best for yourself and your daughter. Leaning on an expert can relieve your fears and guide you through the adolescent wilderness. Jen came to me because she knew she needed emotional support and parent coaching. Jen needed a strategy. Her way wasn't working.

Don't be shy about hiring professionals to help your daughter either. Many of my clients have told me, "The best gift I ever gave myself was hiring a consultant to help my daughter with her college essays." Repeatedly in my practice, I see that the college essay becomes a focal point for family drama. It can trigger anxiety and unworthiness in teens. Why go there when you can hire a professional to help your daughter and let them be the target of your teen's anguish?

You've never needed your community more than when you're parenting a teen on her way to independence. Give yourself permission to put your team together and make life better for you and for your daughter right now.

## Don't Miss These Precious Years

So, what does it look like when a mom is guided by a Powerful Parenting Message, a practice of awareness, and proper outside support? From what I've seen in all my years of practice, it looks like a mom who knows when her daughter needs her to step in and when, as a mom, she needs to step away. Like a mom who can put her monitoring hat aside for a while and enjoy her daughter in the present moment. Like a mom who's able to support her daughter in her best next step, while remaining connected. In other words, a mom who dials down the drama so she can enjoy these precious years with her daughter.

My daughter's senior year was a challenging time for us. One evening, I practically crawled through the front door exhausted from work. All I wanted to do was take a moment for myself and relax. My daughter was lying on the rug in the living room with her laptop open and said, "Mom, watch this video." Pushing through a mountain of resistance, I got on the floor and watched. To my surprise it was Josh Groban, and I loved it, especially because he sang a duet with a woman in the audience.

I joked and said, "That's on my bucket list."

Seconds later I heard, "Mom, come here. Josh is going to be here in Houston next week. We should go."

My first thought was, *I can't*. But then I looked down at her eager face, and this quiet voice said, *She's inviting you into her life. Don't miss this*. Though I'm not a spontaneous person, I said, "Let's go."

A minute later, "Mom, there are two seats in the center on the second row."

I typically get seats on the last row, but I said, "Sure!"

At the show, before we took our seats, my daughter said, "Mom, let's get a picture in front of the stage." As we stood there with our arms around each other, I thought, *When does your senior daughter ever want to get a picture with you?* I treasured this moment and wanted to hold on to it. My heart was so happy throughout the entire concert.

At the end of the show, she turned to me and said, "Mom, aren't you glad you didn't miss this?" I gave her a big hug! I never sang a duet with Josh. But I got something better: this priceless time with my daughter.

When we got back to the car, my daughter plugged back into her world. As she looked down at her phone, I reflected on the last two years. Yes, there were challenges. And I definitely wasn't perfect. But I can honestly say that I didn't miss these precious years with her.

Dear Moms, don't miss these precious years with your daughter either. They are irreplaceable—embrace and cherish them!

## Exercise: Strengthen Your Connection

1   Develop a practice of awareness:

   - Catch yourself obsessing.
   - Recognize when you have your monitoring hat on.
   - Look for times your daughter is trying to connect.
   - And congratulate yourself each time you come into awareness and notice these things.

2   Define your Powerful Parenting Message. Then, think about each phrase of your message and answer these questions:

   - What does living your message look like in real life?
   - Who do you need to be to realize this message?

3 Journal your daughter's positive traits—strengths, character, and abilities—every day for one week. Then reflect on how you feel and write the following down:

- One thing you are grateful for in your daughter.
- One area where you see progress in your daughter.
- One thing you delight in about your daughter.

# 2

# The Maturity Gap...
# Why You're Confused

***

S UE CAME to my office and wanted to talk to me about her daughter Olivia, who was about to graduate from high school. "Where is Olivia going to college?" I asked.

Sue beamed, "Wake Forest University, I'm so proud of her." Then her smile melted away and her face constricted with concern. "To be honest, I'm really apprehensive about Olivia leaving home."

## It's Not Her or You, It's Biology

So many strong emotions are stirred up when your daughter approaches high school graduation. On the one hand, you couldn't be prouder of her. On the other hand, well, you panic that your daughter is ill-equipped to live on her own—a five-alarm fire ignites in your head.

"How can she be ready for college if she can't even clean her room?" Sue exclaimed. "Her room is disgusting—clothes piled high, pizza boxes filled with half-eaten crusts, wet towels thrown everywhere. You can't even see her floor. No one will want to be Olivia's roommate."

The intensity in Sue's voice let me know this was way bigger than her daughter's room. I have seen and heard this intensity hundreds of times when the reality strikes for moms that their daughter is truly leaving. What these moms are really stressing over is some version of the question Sue was asking: "How can my daughter be ready for college if she can't even...

- manage her money?"
- make a phone call?"
- get off social media for two seconds?"
- control her drinking?"
- respect my curfew?"
- get to school or work on time?"
- be respectful and not mean?"

Though the specific worry may differ, these moms share an underlying issue. Each saw areas in their daughter's life that were immature, problematic, and oftentimes disturbing, making them doubt their daughters were ready to leave home.

I asked Sue if there was anything else that was troubling her about Olivia.

"Yes," she said, "Olivia has always been a good kid; she rarely even drinks alcohol. But last week she came home high. The next day I found weed in her room. I couldn't believe it. I feel like I'm running out of time. She's graduating in a month. When I confronted her about the weed, she was angry and mean. She yelled at me, 'I wanted to know what weed was like before I went to college, and you can't do anything about it!'"

"Wow. How did you respond to that?" I asked.

"What can I do?" Sue sighed. "She's going to be on her own in less than three months. What troubles me most, actually more than 'the room,' is her judgment. That was such a dumb decision. What other drugs will she take to prepare for college?"

And then I watched Sue do something that I've seen hundreds of moms do, she turned on herself. She made it personal.

"I wonder what I've done wrong," she said. "It's great that Olivia got into Wake Forest. She's a smart girl, but geez, she's mean, she's a slob, and she has really poor judgment. She's eighteen—isn't she supposed to be an adult? I feel like such a bad mom."

If you feel like Sue, I have good news. You're not a bad mom. All your vacillation about your daughter being ready and not ready for college is not about you. It's just how it is. I'm going to tell you the real situation. It's ambivalent. It's not clear. And nobody is talking about it. But…

## Nothing Magical Happens When You Turn Eighteen

My daughter couldn't wait to turn eighteen so she could be an "adult" and get her first tattoo. I didn't want my daughter to get a tattoo, but I couldn't legally keep her from getting one. I gave her the "this will be on your body forever, are you sure you want one?" talk, but when we sat down for her birthday dinner, she couldn't wait to surprise me and show me her new body art. Yes, I was shocked. It would take a few years before I could appreciate her I'm-now-eighteen tattoo.

This raises a big question. Are you an adult just because you turn eighteen? Neuroscience doesn't think so. Neither do rental car companies. They know that drivers under twenty-five statistically get into more car accidents than other age groups.

What is true is that in the United States, an eighteen-year-old is legally considered an adult and is legally responsible for their behavior. They have many rights. For instance, without parental consent, they can

- vote
- sue or be sued
- open a bank account in their name
- serve on a jury
- have control of their body (i.e., get tattoos and piercings)
- join the military
- marry
- rent a house or an apartment
- make their own medical decisions

Again, do legal rights determine if your son or daughter is an adult? In a December 2016 *New York Times* article by Carl Zimmer, "You're an Adult. Your Brain, Not So Much," Leah Somerville, PhD, a professor of psychology at Harvard University, explains that defining adulthood is not as simple slapping a label on people over age eighteen: "Nothing magical occurs at that age."

Indeed, thanks to recent advances in neuroimaging, research has shown that we don't spontaneously have an adult brain as soon as we turn eighteen. Neurologically, the brain keeps developing well into our twenties.

Scientists agree that the maturing of the brain is a long, complicated process without obvious milestones—it's more a journey than a destination. What's clear is that the changes in your daughter from eighteen to twenty-five are a continuation of the process that started when she entered puberty.

Think of it this way: Your daughter's brain is like a house under major remodeling from puberty to twenty-five. The beginning stages (puberty) are the hardest to handle. Every room is in shambles, and you're dealing with a lot of stress, instability, and chaos. But over time the walls get painted, new appliances are installed, and so on. While many areas of the house (your teen's brain) look finished at eighteen, many areas are still in some level of chaos.

Even this metaphor isn't quite enough. It's evident when a physical house is finished and remodeled; it's not evident when the work on your teen's brain is complete. So therefore, it's really confusing when you're trying to assess your daughter's maturity. Some brain areas are functioning beautifully, others are not.

Though you may not be a neuroscientist, you know intuitively that your eighteen-year-old is not an adult, despite what she thinks or what the legal system decrees. Here's why.

Moms tend to be always working on their mental checklist before their daughter leaves home. You remember when you used to help your ten-year-old daughter pack for camp? You'd work down the checklist. Five pairs of shorts... check. Two sets of sheets... check. Seven pairs of underwear... check. Well, when it comes to our soon-to-be graduating daughters, we have a mental checklist running through our heads. There are many boxes we can check off: Good grades... check. Intelligent... check. But there are many boxes we're just not sure of. Responsible... maybe. Makes good decisions... sometimes. Can manage her life... I hope so. Will do the right thing... help me, God!

See, you know your daughter up close and personal. You know her weaknesses and her vulnerabilities. You also see her strengths and accomplishments. If you're uncertain about letting your precious teen go, it's for good reason. It's biologically impossible to check off all the boxes that would ease your mind and heart. Your eighteen-year-old or even twenty-something daughter does not have an adult brain. The reality is your daughter's brain is both grown up and not quite grown up. Take heart that they're a work in progress. They will mature. But right now, you're dealing with what's known as the Maturity Gap.

## The Maturity Gap

Mom, here's how you experience the Maturity Gap. You watch your daughter perform a perfect grand jeté in her dance recital. You watch your daughter run her heart out for ninety minutes on the soccer field and score several goals. You're amazed at how strong she is and her agility. You're well aware your daughter has a grown-up female body. You keep telling her to wear longer skirts and to hide her cleavage. It's obvious to you that your daughter has physically reached maturity.

And you're amazed at your daughter's cognitive abilities. You've watched her concrete thinking evolve to abstract thinking. You can't believe how she can talk about important issues like systemic racism and how much she understands about politics. You're amazed at your daughter's understanding of complex mathematics and science. You're so proud that she graduated from her IB (International Baccalaureate) program and that she placed out of several classes in college.

But then you find out your daughter sent a nude picture to her boyfriend, and it got spread around school. You're horrified when your daughter stumbles in drunk at 2 a.m. after she drove home from a party. You found out that your daughter stopped going to classes after she got accepted to college and now her high school graduation is in jeopardy.

Moms, this is why you're so confused. There are times you're tricked into thinking your daughter is adult-ish because of her physical and cognitive maturity. But then she does something really careless that seems to sabotage her future. Since you think she's supposed to be an adult at eighteen, you take her actions as proof that you're a bad parent. Mom, it's not you or her. It's the Maturity Gap:

### Physical Maturity + Cognitive Maturity + Emotional Immaturity = The Maturity Gap

Here's another reason it's confusing. In a 2019 article, "Is the Maturity Gap a Psychological Universal?" featured in *Psychology Today*, Lawrence T. White, PhD, had this to say on the subject:

*Studies by developmental psychologists over the past 25 years have identified a general principle: Different human abilities develop at different rates and reach their highest point of development at different ages.*

*For example, the ability to reason in a logical manner increases dramatically from childhood to age 16 or 17 and then levels off. The ability to control one's impulses, however, develops more slowly and over a longer period of time. In fact, most people aren't fully capable of emotional restraint until their mid- or late-20s.*

This is why you may see very different behaviors among your own kids. For example, if you have two daughters, your oldest daughter may have been responsible and easy to trust. It was much easier for you to let her go than your second daughter, who gets in trouble on a consistent basis. This baffles you because you parented them in the exact same way. I know. It's confusing.

Studies have shown that the Maturity Gap appears to be a psychological universal. Around the world, young people reach adult levels of logical reasoning fairly quickly, usually by age sixteen. But these same people struggled to control their impulses, manage their emotions, and resist peer pressure well into their twenties. Why is this? To answer this question, we need to take a look inside the adolescent brain.

## What's Going on Inside the Eighteen- to Twenty-Five-Year-Old Brain?

Going back to the remodeling metaphor, two major areas in the eighteen- to twenty-five-year-old brain are not finished: the principal bedroom and the wiring throughout the house, especially wiring to the principal bedroom. The principal bedroom is the prefrontal cortex (PFC), sometimes called the frontal lobes.

The prefrontal cortex is the master control center of the brain. It helps with social interactions by helping regulate emotions, controlling impulsive behavior, resisting peer pressure, and having empathy. Also, the PFC helps with higher-level cognitive abilities like planning ahead and having a long-term perspective, assessing risks, solving problems, making sound decisions, understanding cause and effect, using good judgment, and giving you cognitive control by suppressing impulses.

Have you ever seen your daughter have a meltdown, make an impulsive decision, do something risky because of peer pressure, use poor judgment, or not think ahead? Yep... any and all of these behaviors are a result of her emotional immaturity and her underdeveloped PFC.

The connections between the differentiated parts of the brain in the adolescent and early-twenty-something brain are like dirt roads. These connections still allow communication (the signal) to travel to widely separated brain regions, but it's slow going. And that delay causes problems.

Here's an example of that delay in action. Your daughter is at a party. The reward center of her brain located in the midbrain and limbic system (often called the lower brain) gets this big shot of dopamine because a guy she likes is there. He gives her a beer and invites her into a bedroom. Sparks are firing in the limbic system, and she says,

"Yes! Let's go for it." In an adult, this yes signal from the limbic system travels efficiently and with great speed up to the PFC. It's like a super-highway; the lower brain and the PFC communicate quickly. Once alerted, the PFC overrides the impulsive and reactive behavior of the lower brain with, "Wait. That's not a good idea. You don't really know him, and he has a reputation of being a player. He's really cute, but *don't* go in the bedroom!" In the immature brain, the yes signal also starts on its way from the limbic system to see what the PFC thinks. But since its pathways have yet to be paved, the signal gets mired in mud and hits a few potholes. As a result, the signal doesn't reach the frontal lobes in time for the PFC to put the brakes on the impulsive and reactive behavior driven by the lower brain. Your daughter doesn't get the "don't" message from the PFC and so goes into the room with the guy.

Throughout adolescence, these dirt roads improve. Over time the connections become "paved" with a substance called myelin, which makes communication more efficient and faster. But the connections don't become finished superhighways until a person's mid- to late twenties.

In her April 2015 *Philadelphia Inquirer* article, "The Teenage Brain You're Sending to College," Dr. Frances E. Jensen states, "research shows that brain connectivity, or how brain regions wire together, is not at all complete at the onset of college, and probably not really done at the end, either. [...] What we all need to realize is that the frontal lobes are key for impulse control, insight, judgment, and empathy, among other things."

You may be wondering what frontal lobes have to do with your daughter. Everything! Just keep reading.

## What the Maturity Gap Looks Like in Your Daughter

Hopefully by now, you're starting to get an idea about what it means that your daughter's PFC isn't fully developed. To bring this home to you even further, let's go function by function through the immature PFC and see—through real-life situations—how each can impact the everyday choices, behaviors, and emotions of young adults. With the exception of the first example, all are from actual college-age clients of mine.

## Decision-Making

With the immature brain, decisions are based on superficial data without careful consideration. Therefore, an immature brain is often not equipped to make good life decisions.

I'm going to tell on myself here. When I was twenty-one, I worked as the photographer at a camp in Colorado for high school teens. One afternoon, I wanted to get some "great pics" of kids white-water rafting. To get my shots, I needed to be on the other side of the river, but there were many things I didn't think through before crossing. I took this rickety swing over a raging river and barely made it across. I didn't consider that there were rattlesnakes on the other side of the river, and I was wearing flip-flops. I walked along a railroad track that hugged a mountain wall and didn't consider that I couldn't hear if a train was coming around the bend because of the loud noise coming from the rapids. After I got my photos, I started walking back along the raging river on the railroad tracks. All of a sudden, I had this hunch to jump off the tracks. As soon as I did, a train came barreling around the corner at ninety miles an hour, literally missing me by a few seconds.

## Judgment

Judgments in the immature brain are often made impulsively, without considering long-term consequences.

Caitlin's best friend at college was Ben. She had no feelings for him and was not sexually attracted to him, but he was her main confidant. After a big party at the sorority house, where Ben had too much to drink, he asked if he could spend the night because he didn't want to drive home. She hesitated because he was being forward with her, but she said yes anyway. Besides, she didn't want him to drive either. That night he wanted to have sex. Caitlin told me in session, "I just let him." She was so upset at herself the next morning and felt like she'd ruined their friendship.

## Impulse Control

In adulthood, cognitive control inhibits impulses. With the immature brain, impulses from the reward center of the brain repeatedly dominate higher-level thinking. In each of these situations, the accelerator (impulse) was stronger than the brakes (PFC).

Chloe couldn't say no to the kolaches, tacos, donuts, and pizza. Before she knew it, she'd gained the freshman fifteen.

Emily ended up having sex with a guy she described as tall and good-looking. She wasn't on birth control and didn't have any condoms. She had sex with him anyway because he was hot. She said she just didn't think about anything... and she got pregnant.

Sara went on a date with Ryan to a fraternity party and can't remember how many beers she had. She said she couldn't stop drinking. She woke up in another guy's bed at the frat house.

Trina couldn't stop texting and harassing her ex-girlfriend. She saw her with another girl on Instagram and was furious. She texted her all night long. Her ex-girlfriend blocked her and told her friends Trina was psycho.

## Social Acceptance

Social acceptance is a core need for all of us. However, for eighteen-to-twenty-five-year-olds this makes them more vulnerable to peer pressure—and not in a positive way. It can cause them to impulsively jump into situations without pausing to assess the risk.

Amy and Bella are both good drivers and normally would never do anything reckless when driving by themselves. However, Amy was devastated over a breakup and wouldn't stop crying. Wanting to cheer her up, Bella cranked up a breakup song on the car stereo, turned the steering wheel as far as it would go, and pressed down on the accelerator. They did more than a hundred donuts in the mall's parking lot singing the breakup song as loud as they could. Not wise. Thankfully, no one got hurt, and Amy did stop crying.

Rosie lived with three other girls in an apartment near the university. Prior to college, Rosie drank alcohol in moderation but was strongly against using drugs. Her roommates smoked weed and did mushrooms. At first Rosie said no, but after a couple of weeks, she joined them. This impacted her motivation and her grades.

## Emotional Regulation

Emotions are hard to control with the immature PFC, so they can override rational thinking and perspective. They can interfere with daily functioning and relationships.

Hannah was a sophomore in college and a great student. She really wanted to go to law school after graduation. Hannah had been dating Noah for more than a year. For nine months, everything was great. But then Noah started pulling away. He made excuses for not hanging out. Hannah started obsessing over Noah all day long. She couldn't focus on preparing for her finals. She couldn't stop thinking, *Why does he avoid me? Why doesn't he care? No one else will be as good to him as I am.* She planned different ways to get his attention. She would call him at 3 a.m., and yell at him for spending too much time on video games, then she'd sob and say, "If you loved me, you would make time for me." Then she'd yell, "Maybe we should just break up!" Then she'd talk to the girls on her hall about Noah and get upset all over again. By allowing Noah to take up the majority of her time and brain space, she ended up doing poorly on all her finals.

## Solving Problems

Often the eighteen-to-twenty-five-year-old has difficulty solving day-to-day problems. Instead of solving the problem, they can procrastinate and avoid.

Amy was a freshman at an expensive private university. Being very social, she went out every night and often missed her morning classes, *which were all her classes.* When she did finally make it to a class, she'd find she was too far behind and didn't know what the professor was talking about. Not knowing what to do about it, she stopped going to her morning classes completely. When her parents asked her how things were going, she lied. Amy made an A+ in her social life, but her parents didn't find out she failed several classes until the end of the school year.

## Not Thinking Ahead

The eighteen-to-twenty-five-year-old has difficulty planning ahead and organizing their behavior to reach a goal. You've seen your daughter struggle with this in high school, and it can continue into the college years and after.

Lexy really wanted to get an internship this summer in neuroscience with her favorite professor, but she missed the deadline.

Madison was supposed to put a deposit down for her apartment for the following year, and she forgot and lost the apartment.

Lilly was a senior in college and needed to sign up for specific classes in order to graduate, but she missed early registration.

## What's Good About an Emerging-Adult Brain

The eighteen-to-twenty-five-year-old brain does have a few advantages over the adult brain. These are the last years of a heightened neuroplasticity that allows your brain to grow easily from experience.

In the same *Philadelphia Inquirer* article I quoted earlier, Dr. Frances Jensen shares,

*The brain's development from late teens to early twenties is nothing short of miraculous. Recent neuroscience has shown us that college-age brains are in sort of a golden period—still with more ability to learn than the adult, as their brain cells are more active and more receptive. Our brain cells, or neurons, and the connections between them, or synapses, can be shaped by experience more readily in the teenage and post-adolescent period than in the adult years. This is termed "synaptic plasticity."*

Repeated use of a synapse during practice causes it to grow and strengthen (molded like plastic by experience), allowing us to learn. The young brain has higher levels of the proteins needed for this process than the adult brain. A stronger synapse means a stronger memory or skill. Remarkably, research has shown that even IQ can change during the teen years—music to the ears of the late bloomers among us.

## Manage Your Expectations, Understand Ambivalence

Understanding where your daughter is developmentally helps you to manage your expectations. I'm definitely not saying that your daughter should stay at home until she is emotionally mature. Her leaving home is good for both you and your daughter.

Just like we can't carry our babies until they can walk perfectly, we can't carry our daughters until they're adults. Babies need to struggle, crawl, pull up, fall, and get back up again before they can walk steadily. And so does your eighteen-year-old daughter. Your daughter has enough emotional maturity to walk, stumble, and fall forward toward adulthood. And college is a good place to do that.

What I can tell you is that your daughter is not going to go through eighteen to twenty-five seamlessly. She will accomplish great things, and she will make mistakes. You will think she is doing great, and then you'll see her fall. You'll think she's finally on her path and be so proud of her, and then she'll go off the rails. Take heart, Mom, all this means is she is still a brain-in-process.

## Letting Go, Holding On

You may have many conflicting feelings after reading this chapter. On the one hand, now that you understand there is a Maturity Gap, it may be harder for you to let your daughter leave. On the other hand, you may find relief because you know you're not alone and you're not crazy.

What is a mom to do with all this ambivalence? Do you let go? Do you hold on? What's your role to play with your eighteen-to-twenty-five-year-old?

You're going to love my answer.

*It depends.* How about that for more ambivalence!

I've talked to so many moms confused about their parenting role, especially in this emerging-adult phase—and for good reason. Your role is in flux. You let go, and you hold on. Your relationship with your daughter is just as important, maybe more, when she leaves home. It, however, will be different and changing.

But take heart, Mom. Because in the next several chapters we go deep and sort through that ambivalence to give you clarity on navigating this developmental period. Having clarity will not only bring you peace, but also strengthen your relationship with your daughter and give you a roadmap for the years ahead. We'll explore what it means to let go. (Believe it or not much of this will be a big relief.) You'll also define and understand the irreplaceable role you're going to play in your daughter's life.

As much as you loved raising your little girl, witnessing your eighteen-year-old evolve into a fully responsible adult woman and getting to support her as she does it is an amazing and rewarding adventure in itself. Some of my most cherished and enjoyable experiences with my daughter have been since she graduated from high school.

## Exercise: Acknowledging the Maturity Gap

I KNOW you may be tempted to skip this exercise, but it will only take twenty to thirty minutes. And it will eliminate a lot of unnecessary suffering...

1   Get out your journal and make two lists:

- List one: Write down the areas where your daughter currently meets your expectations for mature behaviors.

- List two: Write down the areas where you feel your daughter still has some growing up to do.

2   Looking at list two, write down how you'd prefer she behave—your expectations for your daughter in those areas.

3   Now, rewrite your expectations to align with her actual behaviors on list two. For instance, if she's always late, and your current expectation is that she should be on time, rewrite your expectation as: I expect my daughter to be late.

  This doesn't mean you give her a pass on being late, having a messy room, or making a poor decision—you still hold her accountable. What it does mean is that you acknowledge that she's a work in progress. So you expect (not accept) her immature behaviors. And you don't let them upset you or allow you to think there's something wrong with her or your parenting.

4   Revisit this area in your journal every six months or so for the next several years to take heart and note as your daughter's Maturity Gap closes.

# 3

# Letting Go

_____

AFTER MY daughter graduated from high school, she got an apartment close to home. This was the best of both worlds; I got my house back, and I saw my daughter regularly. She had a fifty-five-pound dog named Lilly living in her little studio apartment, and I had a backyard where Lilly could run around, so I was frequently dog sitting. I am a total dog person and so I loved this. And I got to see more of my daughter. I was spoiled.

When my daughter turned twenty, she decided to move to Austin, which is only three hours from where I live. This was not a dramatic move. My sister lives in Austin, and I go there frequently. And yet, when my daughter packed up her car and backed out of my driveway, I thought my heart would break. I went in the house and sat down while the tears rolled down my face. It felt like I would never see her again. But two weeks later, she drove up my driveway and surprised me. We did our typical Whole Foods run. And all felt right in the world.

At twenty-two, my daughter became enamored with Los Angeles. She had several friends who lived there and made a few visits that year. (One of my daughter's special talents is finding cheap flights.) On one of her visits to LA, she called me to tell me she wanted to move there. My heart dropped. But I said that's fine if you can find a decent job.

And she did.

I was happy and proud of her, and yet this felt like a real farewell. My daughter and I have a very close relationship, the only downside being it makes it much harder to say goodbye. But because I love her, I wanted her to have this experience. I love to travel, and I definitely have planted that seed in her heart. I didn't want to hold her back in any way. She was so happy. I didn't want to dampen that.

Her plan was to drive to California with friends. When that fell through, she told me she'd just drive herself. My mother alarm went off for two reasons: 1) Her Subaru Outback had over 150,000 miles on it. And the real reason, 2) I was uncomfortable with her driving there alone. I offered to drive to Tucson with her and visit my friend Sherry. Then my daughter could drive the rest of the way by herself. To my surprise, she said okay.

My daughter was excited about the drive. This was her trip, another rite of passage. And I wanted to support her. This meant I had to let go of a lot of the details—like what time we left, where we stopped, and what we listened to.

She wanted to leave at four in the morning. (Yikes.) So in the pitch dark, we headed west. My daughter drove the first three hours through heavy rain and lightning, playing her electronic music (not my favorite). The sun never came up; the sky went from dark to gray. My daughter and I were both tense because of the stormy weather and bored with the monotonous scenery of West Texas. But she kept playing her music and some of her favorite podcasts, and we both hung in there.

Finally, we broke through the gray as we approached Marfa, Texas, that day's destination. The Davis Mountains were on our right and left, silhouetted against a deep blue sky. Before us was a beautiful orange and red sunset. And right on cue, Spotify played "Ocean" by John Butler Trio, a song that took both of us back to an outdoor music festival in Telluride, where we'd watched an unbelievable performance of it. It was a treasured shared memory.

For those few minutes, time was suspended. Images from our twenty-two years of life together flooded through my mind and heart.

I felt deep gratitude for being her mom and having her as a daughter. I was appreciative of all of it, even the hard stuff. In that moment, I was overtaken with a love so deep and sacred that no words can describe it. I knew then that our love was strong—and we'd be okay.

The next day we ran across the massive dunes in White Sands National Park and drove through another thunderstorm before we got to Sherry's house. After we settled in, we saw a huge rainbow over the mountains. Another sign that my daughter was on the right path.

The next morning my daughter woke me up at 6 a.m. telling me that she was about to drive the last stretch to Los Angeles. I walked her to the car in the rain (again), and she quickly said goodbye.

She drove off, and I could feel the tears coming. It felt like she was driving into the sunset, and I wasn't needed any more. Sherry (who's a therapist too) knew I was sad and suggested we go for a drive. An hour later, we were headed up a mountain covered with forests of saguaro cacti when I noticed my daughter was calling me. I answered, and she said, "Mom, I'm in Phoenix. Ummm... Can you send me money for a cup of coffee? And I also have a flat tire." It's ridiculous at how much joy that phone call brought me. I realized then, at that moment, our relationship wasn't over and I was still needed.

As you can see, letting go was not easy for me, and I know it's not easy for you either. Before I had a teenage daughter, I gave a presentation at the Texas Association for Marriage and Family Therapy Annual Conference and in a very matter-of-fact tone, talked about how teens need to individuate from their parents. But when my daughter was about to leave me, that tone quickly changed. I learned that this "individuation" is *painful* and can feel like a dagger in a mother's heart.

When the day comes for you to say goodbye to your daughter, it may feel paradoxical—completely wrong and completely right at the same time. After all you've poured into your daughter, it feels counter-intuitive to just say "Goodbye." Dropping her off at college or watching her drive away from home can feel like a death.

Take heart, Mom. Think of your goodbye as marking a rite of passage from adolescence to emerging adulthood. This is a transition, not a death. You're not letting go of being a mom, and you're not letting go of the relationship. The truth is that the relationship with your daughter is changing, but the true essence of your relationship will never change, it will only deepen and mature.

## Counting the Days—Real Grief

You may be counting the days until your daughter leaves home because she's been extra cranky and you can't wait to get that negative attitude out of your house. You can't understand why she doesn't want to make the most of her last days at home. At the very same time, you may be counting the days because your heart breaks at the thought of not having her under your roof and being in her life every day.

Your daughter, too, is feeling tension. Likely, there's a constant tug of war going on in her head: "I can't wait to leave." "I'm scared to leave." "I can't wait to be on my own." "I don't want to be on my own." This tension—and the inability of her not yet fully developed brain to process it—produces the crankiness you're noticing. All the huge, complex feelings pulling at her make her an extra edgy, irritable, short-tempered, and argumentative teen (with you and her siblings her frequent targets, no doubt). She doesn't yet know how to let go gracefully and tactfully.

While you long for a deep and meaningful conversation before she leaves, your daughter is laser-focused on the challenges in her immediate future: meeting friends, finding a place to belong, moving into the dorm... She doesn't have the bandwidth to reminisce right now. (Don't worry, these thoughtful conversations will come in their own time once she settles in.)

When your daughter leaves home, expect your emotions to be all over the map—not all negative or all positive. Expect to be genuinely excited for her, as well as a little despondent about family life without her physical presence. Expect to experience real grief and real relief, and sometimes in the same day and even in the same moment.

When my daughter packed her car and backed down the driveway the first time, I did have tears rolling down my cheeks. But an hour later, I called a friend who's gifted in organizing and hired her to help me declutter and reorganize my house. Just thinking about having a clutter-free and orderly house made me happy.

Still, the grief of letting go is real and comes in waves over time. This grief is not a generic feeling like, "I'm sad my daughter has left home." Real grief is specific. It's triggered by the feeling that something that was once ever present in your life is now missing, leaving nothing to replace it, and disrupting the rhythm of the life you've known for eighteen years.

Here's how grief showed up for me:

- I missed seeing my daughter's car in front of my house.

- I missed seeing my daughter in her room looking at her computer.

- I missed the times she'd hop onto my bed and we'd play with the dog or watch a movie together.

- I missed our spontaneous conversations.

- I missed her playing DJ and listening to her music when we'd drive around.

- I missed my shopping buddy, even if it was as mundane as a trip to get groceries.

- I missed being able to look into her eyes or read her body language to know if she was really okay.

- I missed the laughter and energy that filled our house when her friends were over.

I asked my community of moms what they missed when their daughters left home, and here's what they said . . .

- "The late-night open conversations, when she was her most vulnerable and honest. And the sound of her music playing too loud throughout the house."

- "Everything! I miss everything... she's my partner in crime... lunch, shopping, lazy time! I miss our talks."

- "The daily little things: grocery shopping, cooking together, running a Subway sandwich to her at work, going to her track meets."

- "I really miss the conversations. The constant chatter about what is going on in her life."

- "Among other things, I miss her music. She plays piano and clarinet. Suddenly the house was quiet of her rehearsal hours."

- "My daughter joined the navy and just went to Japan. I miss her sweet face every day and hearing her funny stories about school. I even miss the eye rolls I used to get."

- "Watching her dance, the sound of laughter in the house when her 'girl gang' was over, and her hugs."

- "When our family is all together (five girls) now, there's an empty seat at the dinner table. There's an extra space when we gather around the firepit or slide into the church pew."

- "Coffee dates. Coffee is our thing. I just dropped her off last week; coffee isn't the same."

- "The smell of her body sprays lingering after she would dash out the door. Also asking her opinion about what I should wear."

- "I miss our spa/movie nights, when we'd turn on a favorite movie and do facials, mani-pedis, and have girl talk and cuddle up together for a movie."

- "I miss our Saturday afternoons laying out in the sun on our deck, listening to music together. We had some great, meaningful, open conversations this past summer before she left for college."

- "Late-night movies and sleepovers in her room or mine."

- "I really miss seeing my daughter dance. Seems so simple, but I was so very involved with all of her dance from age three to eighteen... then she ended up as a dance major on the other side of the country."

- "Lazy Saturday mornings when she would crawl into bed with me and chat about all the random things going on in her life and world."

- "I miss unstoppable laughter watching our favorite shows together. I miss spa days at home, coffee dates, baking together. I miss seeing her 'stuff' around the house and driving up and seeing her car in the driveway. I miss goodnight talks."

- "I missed her baked goods, her fun interactions with her brothers, and mostly her energy in our family. You don't realize how different your family dynamics will be when one person leaves!"

- "I miss her laughing and just being funny, and our mommy-and-me dates! Our impromptu shopping trips were awesome too."

This is only a sampling of the many responses I received. What's clear to me from all these replies is moms experience real grief, and it shows up in ways unique to each mother-daughter relationship.

## Real Relief

Just like there's real grief, however, there's also real relief. Most likely, you've already experienced some of the relief of your daughter transitioning into young adulthood. For instance, she graduated from high school and she's really going to college. Actually, this is more than a relief; it's cause for celebration.

Grief and relief can be very closely connected, like two sides of a coin. Once your daughter has moved into her dorm or new apartment, you may notice that while you miss her, you're more at ease without her at home. You have fewer distractions and interruptions, and more time. You have energy to give to your career and creative projects. You have room for new opportunities.

As much as you loved and miss your daily connection with her, you're finding there are a lot of things you don't miss. You don't miss the daily struggles with screens and curfews. You don't miss the stressed-out daughter who directed her drama at you or her siblings. You don't miss the wet towels on the floor or her dishes in the sink. You don't miss having to stay up until one in the morning to make sure she made it home okay.

Also, there is a relief in being a tad clueless and not knowing all her day-to-day thoughts, decisions, and moods. Sure, you loved knowing the daily details of her life, but, if you're being honest, it gave you so much more to worry about... like when you know she's upset about her boyfriend or you know the crowd she's out with is the party crowd. Not knowing brings its own kind of peace.

## The Real Challenge: Letting Go of Control

Letting go is a process. And one you've had practice with and been successful with already. You've been letting go of control a little at a time since your daughter was a wee one.

My earliest memory of letting go happened when my daughter was three years old and decided she wanted to dress herself and pick out her own clothes. I used to love to put her in cute girly dresses; I didn't want to give that up. But my daughter was adamant that she choose her outfit, which typically was either a tutu or a long princess dress. At first, her choices bothered me (the grief). But I had to admit that her being able to dress herself made things easier for me, and for that I was grateful (the relief).

By the time your daughter has turned eighteen, there've been countless times you've let go of control. With each release, you've experienced the grief and the relief of letting go. Even with the tiny changes, there's a risk involved making it hard to release her—thankfully, our daughters are adept at pushing us to do so. Mom, the truth is all these "letting gos" have made you stronger and have prepared you for the real challenge of letting go when your daughter moves out.

## Retiring the Monitor

For eighteen years you've been monitoring your daughter to make sure she

- gets to school and practice on time,
- is on top of her studies,
- is being responsible on social media,
- is hanging out with the right friends,
- helps around the house and keeps her room clean,
- drives responsibly and makes curfew,
- and a thousand other things...

You probably monitored her right up to the minute before she left home. "Dear, don't forget to bring... Did you pack your...?"

And now what's a *monitor* to do?

Monitoring has been an important part of your parenting. It was needed. But now you need to shift your approach with your daughter. It's time the monitor retires. I know this is challenging. It means huge changes in every aspect of your more-than-eighteen-year relationship. But this needs to happen for your sake, your daughter's sake, and your relationship's sake.

Practically speaking, you need to retire the monitor because you physically *can't* monitor your daughter any longer. She's not in your home. You can't get her out of bed, feed her, choose her friends, dress her, make sure she acts responsibly at a party, and stand over her to supervise her homework. You can't chain yourself to her... she is living on her own.

But more important, you need to retire the monitor because your daughter needs the freedom to find her own way and make her own choices. Your daughter needs to discover more of her true self and personality—so she can monitor herself.

My own daughter told me, "No one knows who they are until they leave home. They learn to be autonomous on their own."

## Welcoming the New Monitor—
## Your Maturing Daughter

Last year, when my daughter was twenty-four, we went grocery shopping for Thanksgiving dinner. She'd volunteered to do the majority
of the cooking, and I was really grateful. I had my list, and I had my
game plan on how to shop.

A few minutes in, I could tell my daughter was getting irritated
with me, and I realized that she had her own game plan. This was a
new realization for me. My daughter had *her own way* of grocery shopping. I was tempted to make her do it my way, but she was cooking…
and I wanted to support her emerging-adult self. Now, my job was to
step back and respect her way.

Your daughter, too, needs space to find her way in all the different
areas of her life. This is not easy for moms. We want our way even
in the small things. Some may call this micromanaging. But in our
minds, it's "helping her," "doing what's best." However we label it,
chances are our daughters find it really annoying as they struggle to
come into their own and take responsibility for their lives.

Your daughter's way will often be different from yours. Sometimes
it will really press your buttons. But just as your letting go is a process
and not always a pretty one, finding her way is a process for her as
well and can be messy. In fact, expect it to be messy. And expect your
daughter to keep experimenting until she finds her way.

Some of these "experiments" will be small and have nothing to do
with her safety and well-being. They won't jeopardize her future. For
example, she may cut off her beautiful long hair or dye it green. Maybe
she gets a facial piercing. She may change her clothing style to one
you abhor and even disapprove of. And yes, she will have regrets. But
all of this is good fodder for finding her way. It is also good fodder for
you to build your "non-monitoring" muscle for when the stakes are
higher and it's harder for you to stay silent.

There are many important areas where your daughter is working
to find her way:

- finding a core group of friends
- dating and sexuality
- tending to her basic needs of eating, sleeping, exercising, and rest
- belonging to a group and getting involved in her community
- cultivating a spirituality and nurturing her soul
- managing her studies and schedule
- finding meaningful work and career

Her active searching—trying different things—in all those areas is how your daughter learns who she is and how to monitor herself, her choices, her decisions, her time, and her money so she can become an adult. Just as she would never have learned to dress herself or form friendships or drive a car if you had always done these things for her, your daughter can't learn to monitor herself if you're always there with the answer.

## Monitoring in Disguise: Prying and Unsolicited Advice

When you love your daughter and you're curious, it's all too easy for your seemingly innocent questions to morph into prying and become prompts for unsolicited advice. So, be aware: As reasonable as inquiring about your daughter's day and letting her know what you think seem to you, both can create a slippery slope into monitoring. That's not good for your relationship.

What are you doing tonight? Who is going to be there? Where are you going? Who is going to drive? Have you done your homework? What did you eat today? Have you met anybody you like? Where did you meet him? Have you gone out? How many times? What's his major?

These aren't bad questions. But they become prying when you frequently bombard her with them and when you demand that your daughter tell you now, on your timetable, instead of waiting for her to open up to you.

When you ask, "Have you been studying?" she assumes you think she's *not* studying, and that you have an agenda to get her to study. If you ask her, "How much did you drink at the party?" she assumes you think she's binge drinking and your agenda is to get her to stop drinking. In both cases, she's probably right.

I asked a good friend what the hardest thing about being a mom of a girl in college is, and she said, "Keeping my mouth shut."

Truth.

Knowing when not to talk or question is very challenging for moms. Your daughter tells you how she's going out on all these dates and having so much fun, and all you hear is that she's neglecting her studies. So you use this information she's shared with you as an opportunity to give her your unsolicited advice. "You can't be going out every night of the week. You should be studying. We didn't spend all this money on your tuition for you to party all week."

Now, Mom, I don't disagree with you. Your concern is good. It's just that your approach *won't work*. Your questions won't pry out of her the answers you're looking for. Instead, you'll get a defensive response. She'll shut down, give you one-word answers, or won't return your texts or calls. And her annoyance at your not responding to what she's saying but using what she shares to give unsolicited advice will prevent her from hearing anything you have to say. Instead, she'll bristle and tune you out. (The following chapters tell you how to give advice that gets heard.)

## Honor Your Fear and Anxiety

I love this quote from Elizabeth Gilbert: "You are afraid of surrender because you don't want to lose control. But you never had control; all you had was anxiety."

See, the monitor wants to control, but you really don't have control; all you have is anxiety. And this unbridled anxiety is in charge, causing the monitor to be *out of control*. It causes urgency, panic, and obsessive thoughts. It hijacks all your attention. It sets off the sympathetic nervous system and triggers your stress response, cutting you off from the strategic, problem-solving part of the brain.

"So," you ask, "am I just supposed to ignore my anxiety?"

No. You want to honor it. Only through honoring your anxiety—acknowledging it—can you work through it so it doesn't result in crippling fear and behaviors (like monitoring) that you want to release.

Let's recognize that we moms are justifiably scared for our daughters. As we know now, there is the Maturity Gap. Which means we also now know our daughters don't always make the best decisions and choices. And that's when our mother's intuition kicks in and alerts us that something is not quite right. You have a sense that your daughter is off track. And much of the time your mother's intuition is spot-on.

You feel anxious because your fears are real. Will my daughter be okay? Is she safe? Is she ruining her future? Will I lose her? What will happen to our relationship? Let's also recognize that our fears and anxiety are coming from a good place. You have this fierce protective instinct because you love your daughter and want her to be okay.

We honor the truth of our anxiety by sitting with it and bringing it into our awareness. Too often when we feel something is off, we just get busier. Ignoring your feelings won't make them go away; it'll actually make them bigger.

Instead, take a break. Find a place where you won't be distracted. You need quiet to catch up with your thoughts and feelings. Grab a journal and start with your burning question, like, "What's going on with me? What am I feeling right now?" Then set a timer for fifteen minutes and write. Whatever you write is perfect. Don't edit or judge yourself. Afterward, see if you can identify your specific fear or worry.

What really helped me was writing down every little worry I had about my daughter. Try the same. Here are some examples:

- I worry she's smoking weed.
- I worry she'll get pregnant.
- I worry she'll fail her classes.
- I worry she'll get in a car accident.

After you've made a comprehensive list of worries, turn each one around into a prayer or an intention. What's very important is that your prayer or intention use positive imagery. You don't want your prayer to be "Don't let my daughter get raped." That's a horrible image and will only increase your anxiety. Instead, turn it around with a positive image: "I pray that my daughter is protected all through the day and night," or, "I see my daughter protected all through the day or night."

The positive images can help calm your anxiety.

If you're worried your daughter is doing drugs, perhaps use this prayer: "I pray that my daughter is healthy and free of all addictions." Or turn it into an intention or visualization: "I see my daughter healthy and free of all addictions."

Again, take every worry on your list and turn it around to create your list of prayers or intentions. Then, say them once a day.

Here's why this is helpful: This transforms your worry and anxiety into something positive and useful. It shifts the negative images that increase anxiety and helps you focus on positive images that are good and healthy for your daughter. This can free you from being ensnared by anxiety.

## You Still Have a Role to Play

The monitor's motto is to "Let go and let Mom" instead of "Let go and let God." But nothing productive comes out of "Let go and let Mom." I know first-hand. When I fall into that trap, my shoulders and back hurt. I feel burdened, sad, preoccupied, stressed, and drained. My cortisol levels skyrocket. None of this helps my daughter or our relationship.

Our parenting role as mothers of young adult daughters is changing and maturing as our daughters are. But always, our most important responsibility to our daughters—no matter how old or independent they get—is to protect and continue our connection to them. Yes, it will be different, and you will miss her daily presence in your home. But what you'll find is when you're mentally prepared for that change and you're able to retire the monitor, your relationship with your daughter will become more enjoyable and you'll grow even closer.

## Exercise: Taming Your Inner Monitor

NEXT TIME you feel worried about your daughter, instead of picking up the phone, pick up your journal.

1   Write your worry down.

2   Then turn it around. Phrase it in positive language in the form of a prayer or intention. (Example: If your worry is "Someone will slip my daughter a drug and rape her," turn it into "My daughter is wise and knows not to leave a drink unattended, and she is protected and surrounded by good people who care about her.")

3   Set a timer for three minutes and repeat your positive intention to yourself over and over until the timer rings.

Make this and other positive intentions you've created concerning your daughter part of your morning or evening ritual, as needed.

# 4

# Five Key Facets for Laying a New Foundation

ICHELLE'S TWENTY-YEAR-OLD daughter, Alyssa, is a sophomore at the University of California, Los Angeles. Michelle
lives in Houston. "It was especially hard saying goodbye to
Alyssa this year," Michelle told me during our session, "We're
so close, and now she's halfway across the country."

"Wasn't she at UCLA last year?" I asked.

"She was," said Michelle. "But last year, we talked every day. We
still talk a lot, but it feels like she's not telling me everything. She feels
farther away than she did last year. Does that make sense?"

I nodded.

"Alyssa has a big heart. Everybody wants to be her friend," Michelle
continued. "But I worry. She's a business major, and this year she's
taking some difficult courses. I get the sense that she's more focused
on her social life than her studies."

"Tell me about your last conversation with Alyssa," I prompted.

"Perfect example," said Michelle. "Alyssa has been playing a lot of
golf lately. Her friend Tyler keeps inviting her. Last week they played
eighteen holes—twice! So when I called Alyssa this week and she told
me she'd just gotten back from playing golf with Tyler, I thought I'd

explode. I just kept thinking, *She's going to fail all her classes.* What came out of my mouth was, 'You're playing golf *again*?!' She got quiet after that. But I don't know what to do. What's my role here? Do I let her fail?"

I know, Mom... this is hard. Most mothers would have said the same thing. Michelle didn't say anything wrong. She didn't blatantly attack her daughter. But Alyssa got the message. She knew "you're playing golf *again*?!" was code for "you're not studying enough." Michelle had defaulted to her monitor role, and Alyssa immediately recognized her old nemesis. She felt judged. Her response was to avoid the monitor (aka, Mom). And she could, because now she doesn't live at home.

So where does that leave Michelle and all moms with twenty-something daughters? It leaves us in transition. We know we must retire the monitor. But we don't always know how to do so or even what that looks like.

As we talked about, the monitoring facet of parenting takes on greater importance during a child's teen years out of necessity. Other facets of parenting—empathy, understanding, and all those things we love about the role—while still there, aren't front and center. You may even have discounted them for the sake of enforcing important boundaries for your teenager.

But now as your daughter teeters on adulthood, it becomes imperative that the monitoring facet is set aside and some softer facets of parenting return to center stage. Your consistent use of them becomes foundational to creating and maintaining a strong, healthy, and genuine heart connection with your daughter.

Be aware, however, that the softer facets of your parenting her in childhood need updating—the time for healing boo-boos with a kiss and solving everything with a hug and a sticker has passed. As her world and its challenges become more complex, she needs your love and support in a different way. You can make sure you're there for her fully by integrating the following five key facets into your parenting practice moving forward.

FACET 1
# Parenting the Heart: Be Her Home Base

Do you remember playing tag? Where you'd keep running hither and thither to avoid being caught? The only place you were safe and could catch your breath was on home base.

You want to be your daughter's home base now, a place where she can rest. A place where she can be herself and remember who that is. She's going to need that periodically.

When your daughter goes to college, she's totally out of her comfort zone. Everything is new, and while that's wonderful, it's also emotionally exhausting because "new" makes the brain work harder. She's likely to find herself competing to get into classes, make the team, and make new friends—unsure where she fits and how she stacks up in this unfamiliar environment.

A beautiful college girl once told me, "I can't believe he's interested in me—every girl in the sorority house is smart, beautiful, and thin." In a competitive environment, you feel like you have to be always on—that's stressful. It takes a lot of energy to find your group of friends and a place to belong. And that path is often not a smooth one. Your daughter may get caught up in trying to be or act a certain way in order to fit in. It's easy for these girls to lose themselves and get off track.

When you are there as her home base, your unconditional love for her provides a safe haven from the world. Your daughter knows she can take a break from all that competition. She can rest with someone she knows has seen her at her worst yet still loves and accepts her and expects nothing more from her than to be who she is. Just knowing you're always there for her gives her the security to move through the world with more confidence.

As her home base, you also act as a touchstone that allows her to remember where she came from and reminds her who she is at her core.

I'm a native Houstonian and went to the University of Houston for my undergraduate degree. I didn't really leave familiar surroundings until I went to the University of Arkansas (UA) to get my master's degree. UA accepted me to be an associate head resident for a freshman dorm. I was in charge of twelve student advisors. So I was well planted. I had instant community and purpose.

But I didn't know one person there. I was making all new friends. I'll never forget the feeling of no one *really* knowing me. No one knew my history. There was no reference point. No inside jokes. That feeling was very disorienting.

I was far enough away that I couldn't go home on the weekends. So I'd call my family and long-time friends. I'd share my stories and my parents would share normal day-to-day minutiae. This—touching my home base even through a phone—was enough to help me feel normal.

Don't worry, Mom. Your daughter doesn't come back to home base to stay. She comes back to catch her breath, to center herself, to gather her strength before she gets back in the game. Your job now is to be that refuge—whether in person, over the phone, or simply in her mind.

## FACET 2
# Be Her Anchor—Put Things in Perspective

Because of her underdeveloped brain, your daughter will often default into all-or-nothing thinking, like, "I didn't get the internship. Nothing works out for me." Or, "I never go out." Or, "I'm failing everything."

As your daughter's anchor, you are strong and immovable—there for her to turn to and lean on no matter what life throws at her. As a full-grown adult with a fully mature brain, you know that rarely is a situation all or nothing. So it's up to you to help her see that. Without judgment, you help her put things in perspective. Without being a Pollyanna, you remind her of the positives in her life. You help her to quantify her story and see things in context. (If your daughter is emotionally flooded, wait until she calms down to put things in perspective.)

When you're in anchor mode, your conversations might go something like:

*Daughter: "I didn't get the internship. Nothing works out for me."*

*You, acknowledging her feelings but also remembering the positive:*
*"I know that's disappointing. Honey, I know you will find another internship. Remember, you had a great internship last summer, and your supervisor wrote you a great recommendation. Your grades are good."*

*Daughter: "I never go out!"*

*You, quantifying her story: "I know it may feel that way. You have at least six good friends who really love you. Last weekend you went to the lake house with three of them. And the week before, you were home and went out with Camilla and Taylor."*

*Daughter: "I'm so stupid. I'm making a C in organic chemistry."*

*You, putting things in context: "You know organic chemistry is one of the hardest classes at your college. It's just a very challenging course. Remember you have As in the rest of your classes."*

Putting things in perspective also means helping her shift her focus from outcome to process. Your daughter will have disappointments, failures, and roadblocks. She will make poor choices. As does every other human on the planet.

You put these life hiccups in perspective for her by continually praising her process no matter the outcome. When she fails, praise her for getting back up. When she's scared, praise her for doing it anyway. When she tries something new, praise her for going out of her comfort zone. When she takes action, praise her even if—especially if—it's imperfect action. For instance, you might say,

- "I'm so proud of you for continuing to try out for the dance company after you were rejected last fall. You never gave up. You continued to take dance classes, and you've done the hard work."

- "I'm proud of you for contacting your professor and asking for extra help."

- "I'm proud of you for going to the fraternity party even though your ex-boyfriend was there."

- "I'm proud of you. It took a lot of courage to set a boundary with your friends."

- "I'm proud of you. It took a lot of courage to make an appointment with the therapist."

- "I'm proud of you. It took a lot of courage to tell me about your girlfriend."

When you consistently draw attention to her competence in the process, you help her evolve out of black-and-white thinking. You help her see issues for what they are. You help her realize her own resiliency, courage, and strength. Most important, your praise shows her that she's more than capable of handling what comes her way, so eventually, she can become her own anchor.

## A Friendly Reminder: Anchors Stay Put

As your daughter is tossed about in the turbulent emotional storms of young adulthood, remember you are her anchor—not her copilot. It's easy for us moms to get swept away in our children's emotions, so you must prepare yourself to stand steady for your daughter. Letting her pull you into her drama does her no good, and you're the one who ends up stressed.

I've heard this scenario a thousand times and have experienced it with my own daughter. You're relaxed and having a great day when you see that your daughter is calling you. This makes you so happy. You answer the phone. And the next thing you know, you're in the middle of a big emotional dump:

"Mom, I hate my roommate. She's so weird and mean. I can't sleep or study in my room when she's here."

Or, "Mom, everyone in my sorority just wants to party every night. My best friends are in the other sorority. I want to quit mine."

Or, "Mom, I'm so fat. I hate myself. I don't want to go out anymore."

And before you can open your mouth, your daughter says, "Mom, I gotta go."

*Whaaaat?!*

Your day is ruined. Now you're stressed out of your mind and are obsessing over your daughter. You text her to tell her to call you back. An hour later, she calls. She's moved on and says, "It's fine, Mom!"

*Really?*

It's that easy to get pulled into your daughter's drama storms. Those stormy phone calls result from her immature brain's inability to put things in perspective. The slightest thing happens, and she goes right into stress response because her reactive brain didn't connect with the higher problem-solving part of the brain. She doesn't need you to join her craziness; she needs you to be her anchor—to put things in perspective, to praise her process, and to let her know she can make it through this storm as well as the next.

## FACET 3
## Be the Voice of Empathy

Recently, my client Shelly told me that Abby, her twenty-year-old daughter, called her and said, "Mom, I don't need a solution; I really need to be heard." She then went on to tell her mom that she bombed her statistics test, and that she had several more big tests that week but couldn't concentrate.

"Sounds like you're really shaken up after taking the statistics test," said Shelly. "And you're scared because you have two more big tests this week. I can understand how you'd feel overwhelmed."

I was proud of Shelly. She could have jumped straight into solution or panic mode. But she listened to Abby and reflected back what she heard with empathy. Mom's response helped to soothe Abby's distress.

We all want to be understood. None of us likes being fixed. Think about you and your partner. How do you feel when you pour your heart out to your husband and he tells you what to do? It probably makes you mad, even if he's right. You want to be understood first and so does your daughter.

When your daughter trusts that you'll respond with empathy, she'll open up to you. When she knows you'll handle whatever she has to say without freaking out, she's more likely to share her worst fears, confident your empathy and understanding will calm her stormy waters.

By your extending empathy (instead of judgment or advice), she can contain her anxiety in your groundedness. You are supporting her with your strength and resolve until she finds her own.

Your daughter does need to hear the voice of reason (that's the next chapter), but she won't be able to listen until she has heard the voice of empathy.

## FACET 4
# Be Her Mirror

When you are anchored (and not reactive) and consistently respond with empathy, you become a mirror for your daughter. Your response reflects her experience back to her and lets her know that she has been truly seen.

Your judgment, monitoring, and agenda are no longer part of your interactions. Through your words, presence, and energy, you communicate that everything she feels is okay and no part of her is too much. From there, she can form a healthier sense of self.

This is one of the biggest gifts you can ever give her because there can be a great deal of distorting and negative mirrors in your daughter's life with friends and dating. These can have big negative consequences for her well-being. Your daughter can be surrounded with hundreds of people, but if she doesn't accurately feel seen or felt by anybody, she can experience a crippling loneliness.

In his book *Brainstorm: The Power and Purpose of the Teenage Brain*, world-renowned neuroscientist Dr. Daniel Siegel states, "When we feel that another person feels our feelings, that can be called 'feeling felt.' This feeling is one of the most important aspects of a close and supportive relationship." Your mirroring or tuning in to your daughter not only reflects that you see her but enables her to "feel felt" by you.

Being her mirror is also one of the biggest gifts you can give yourself. It keeps you attentive to what she's saying and what she's not saying. You're aware of her nonverbal cues. You can sense when she is elated and when something's off. Being a healthy mirror for your daughter is a powerful way to guard against her developing loneliness, depression, anxiety, and hopelessness. As good mirror, whether near or far, you hold all the parts of your daughter's soul.

## FACET 5
# Be Her Encourager in Chief—See the Good

Seeing the good in our daughters should be easy, right?

Unfortunately, no. Remember the Powerless Parenting Message? If you haven't already changed it, now is the time.

I'm going to tell on myself again. After my daughter had been in California for about six months, she told me she'd lost her Texas driver's license. She said she thought someone had it when she'd been in Northern California.

If this sounds vague, it's because it was vague. And our brains hate open loops. Brains tend to obsess about things that aren't complete. For me, that was the lost driver's license. I obsessed about it. And I didn't do it quietly.

I'd bring it up to my daughter every time we talked, only to get another elusive answer or get ignored. This went on for months. That lost license was all I could think about. Why didn't she ask her friend if she found it? Why didn't she report it missing and get another one? She could get arrested. Or worse, someone could be using it and get arrested with her identity. (See what I mean? Obsessed.)

I then tried what I thought was a creative angle. I texted her about her license. She went ballistic. At that point, I finally got the message from God, the universe, and legions of angels to *let it go*.

Now of course my daughter needed to get a driver's license, but I wasn't helping things. Not so miraculously, when I backed off, she came up with a plan. She flew back to Texas and got a new license.

The problem here is that I was definitely not her encourager. I was a very pesky fly (maybe even a mosquito). All my attention was on the driver's license. When she called, I went straight to the license issue. I didn't hear—because I wasn't listening for—any of the good she was doing. And there was a lot of good. My daughter was working hard in school, had started a successful business, and was building a community of friends.

Don't be a pesky fly.

As her encourager, you look for the good in your daughter and keep your attention there. You want to focus on what your daughter is doing right. Her gifts, characteristics, and abilities. This doesn't come naturally to most of us, so you'll likely need to practice. A great question to ask every day is, "What's good about my daughter?" And then tell her. Send her a random text starting with, "I really appreciate..." She'll love it.

## Guidelines for the New Connection— The Don'ts and Dos

Now that you know the key facets of parenting that need to be rekindled as your daughter moves toward young adulthood, here are some "Don'ts and Dos" that tell you what to look for and what to beware of as you put these facets into action.

### Don't Make It All About You

You make it all about you when you take things personally.

No mom raises her hand and says, "I want to take things personally." It happens when you forget that your daughter is developmentally immature. You need to remember: Her mistakes are not *your* failure. They are her mistakes.

If you get hurt because your daughter forgets your birthday or she hasn't returned your call, it's understandable and needs to be addressed. But it's not personal. Again, it's typical behavior for her age group. She is still a work in progress.

Remembering this will save you a lot of needless suffering. Taking things personally is a huge time waster and not useful.

### Don't Become Enmeshed

Enmeshment results from poor boundaries between you and your daughter. You lose your life because you're completely consumed with hers. You feel her feelings like they're your own. You become absorbed with her problems to the point they become yours. You find satisfaction by living vicariously through your daughter's experiences.

Drama and enmeshment go hand in hand. Remember the movie *My Big Fat Greek Wedding?* There was lots of family drama. Poor Toula couldn't make a move without all of her family being up in her business. Yep. Enmeshment.

Enmeshment is not healthy for you, and it's annoying to your daughter. You get to have your own life, and your daughter gets to have hers.

## Don't Try to Change Her

Often, we dream of having a baby girl who'll grow up and be just like us. This rarely happens. Our daughters tend to be very different from us. And this is a good thing. I didn't like Barbie dolls. However, my daughter had more than fifty of them, and I never bought her one. I am a peacemaker and very diplomatic. My daughter speaks her mind and doesn't hold back. We're different.

I would hate to make my daughter a mini-me. Yes, it's hard seeing our daughters make different choices than we'd make—with clothing, hair color, opinions, spirituality, politics, friends, music, hobbies, and careers. But we need to give our daughters the space to find out who they are and what they believe. Most importantly, we need to lay our judgments aside. If your daughter feels you're trying to change her, she will build a wall between you.

I respect my daughter for so many things: She's good in science. She actually loves anatomy and physiology. I'm good in the social sciences, but not that kind of science. I respect her *because* she is different from me.

## Do Connect on a Consistent Basis

You want to stay current with your daughter on a consistent basis, whether that means by text, FaceTime, or phone. There are some who would say you need to FaceTime your daughter once a week. I believe it's more organic than that, especially with girls. The main principle here is to take the lead from your daughter. It's not about what you need; it's about what she needs.

There will be times she needs you more because she feels more vulnerable. She may be struggling with roommates or with confidence and need a little more reassurance. My client Sheila's daughter is a dance major who was having an especially hard time during auditions. She talked to her mom on the phone at least once a day for a couple of weeks—which was needed. After the auditions, they went back to speaking every few days.

However often you talk, you can deepen the connection by sharing something about your life with your daughter. It could be something that happened at work, a new recipe you tried, a new song you learned on the piano, or that you were able to do a handstand in yoga class. It could be mundane or entertaining. This allows her to know you beyond the monitor. It helps her see you as a person. And because you're not scrutinizing her, she can freely share something back with you.

If connecting becomes difficult, send a lighthearted or playful text to get her attention. When she responds, let her know you'd love to catch up and ask her when she has time. If she texts back saying, "Mom, I'm swamped this week with classes," let her know that's fine, you can talk next week.

In the meantime, send her encouraging texts, like, "I am so proud of you for how hard you've been studying." Send her something that would make her smile, like a silly cat or dog picture. Send texts that don't require a response but that affirm the relationship, like, "Thinking about you" and "Love you so much."

If your daughter doesn't reply to your initial request to catch up, and you start to panic, just own your worry. Text her something like, "Hey Dear, I haven't heard from you in a while, and I'm starting to worry about you. Can you send me a text and let me know you're okay?" (With a heart emoji.)

## Do Give Her Space and Freedom

Your daughter needs her space and freedom. Your baby bird is finally out of your nest and needs some time to find her wings. It's a time of exploration. She's coming into her own. Give her time to figure out her way of managing her life with all her trials and errors. When you give her space and freedom, you know when she calls or asks you to come visit it's because she wants to and she's ready.

You also want to give her space and freedom in your conversations. Moms love details. But if your daughter is not ready to talk about her new boyfriend or soccer or whatever, take her lead. Don't pry. You can throw out a question, but if she doesn't take the bait, just let it be. She needs some time. Again, when she's ready, she'll voluntarily tell you everything you want to know.

## Do Share Positive Adventures

You have a unique opportunity when your daughter is eighteen-to-twenty-five years old. She has a lot of freedom and no money. She's been on her own enough to appreciate the gift of travel with you. (Not like those high school years when all she did was complain and text her friends when you took her to the Big Apple.) If you have the key facets in place, she'll gladly accept your offer to go on an adventure together. These times are priceless. They create memories of a lifetime and bring you closer.

I hadn't been back to the University of Arkansas since I received my master of fine arts degree. But one fall, not too long ago, I decided to go to Fayetteville to see the leaves. My daughter loves fall, especially when the leaves are changing. (We don't experience fall in Houston.) I asked her if she'd like to go with me—and she said, "Yes!"

It was so much fun for me to walk around the campus with my daughter. Much had changed but not the art building. It was as dingy as I remembered it. The maple leaves were outstanding—golden yellows, deep reds, and intense oranges.

My daughter wanted to draw with me someplace I'd gone as a graduate student. I took her to Devil's Den State Park, where I had done a whole series of fall paintings for my thesis show many moons ago. It was sunny and perfect weather. We sat next to a stream surrounded by vibrant-colored trees, both of us with our sketchbooks on our lap and pastels in hand trying to capture the beauty. My daughter would ask me for help every once in a while, but mostly we sat in silence, happy and content to be experiencing this together. This is something we will never forget.

## The Move to Friend-*Like* Status

As you incorporate these five key facets of parenting into your relationship with your daughter, you're likely to find your interactions transforming—and for the better. You're likely to find you're becoming more "friend-like."

Of course, your daughter won't be your best friend. She can't be your confidant. She won't be there for you like your best friend is, but she will become friend-like in the most wonderful ways.

As your daughter matures and your monitor retires, you'll find yourself more relaxed around her, more yourself and not just her mother. If she's nearby, you'll find you really enjoy her company—in a very different way than when she was younger. Even if you aren't in the same location, you'll notice your communication becomes more friend-like. There's a playful and sometimes silly tone to the texting. You share photos and memes that make you both laugh.

An old picture came up on my Facebook feed the other day. It was taken when my daughter first learned to drive. She'd parked at Target as far away from the other cars as possible, and I think we had to walk a half a mile to get to the store. So I sent the photo to my daughter, and it made her smile.

There are times that you may be the "filler" friend for your daughter, and that's okay. When your daughter is feeling lonely or left out, she might FaceTime you. If you ask your daughter what's going on, and she says, "Nothing," but she keeps chatting, know that you are her filler friend. Don't think of this is as a waste of time. You're satisfying a need for her. She needs someone to hang out with—who better than her trusted home base? Just cherish the time with her.

When you experience this friend-like stage, you'll know you've successfully retired the monitor and set a firm foundation for the next phase of your mother-daughter journey.

## Exercise: Preparing Yourself

TO PREPARE YOURSELF to reawaken those softer key facets of parenting in a more mature way and reinforce the "Don'ts and Dos," try these exercises:

1 To remind yourself that your daughter is a work in progress, write WIP on your calendar on your birthday, Mother's Day, and any other special day. Then, when the day comes and she forgets to reach out, remind yourself her forgetfulness is not a reflection on your parenting or a measure of how much she loves you. She is a work in progress. If she does remember, praise her and tell her how much it means to you.

2 List your daughter's traits that are different from yours. Circle the ones you respect. Then tell your daughter how much you admire these abilities.

3 Write down one thing to share about yourself the next time you speak with your daughter. Then share it.

4 Plan a small adventure and invite your daughter to join you—you will not regret it.

# 5

# The Consultant

ELEN PUT the five key facets to work when her daughter Brianna left for Southern Methodist University (SMU) in-Dallas—four hours from their home in Houston.

She texted and FaceTimed Brianna throughout the week. And she made home a place Brianna was happy to retreat to a couple of times a semester to regroup and get the love and support she needed.

Helen was Brianna's touchstone.

Brianna would call in complete meltdown. "I'm going to fail my biochemistry midterm. I'll never get into med school." When that happened, Helen would help her put things in perspective. "That's exactly how you felt after your physics exam and you made an A, remember?" Brianna would relax.

Helen was Brianna's anchor.

And when Brianna got all dressed up in her cute black dress and heels, and was ghosted—after she'd told everyone about her amazingly gorgeous date—she called her mom in tears. Helen sat with her in her pain and said, "I'm so sorry. What a terrible thing for him to do. This must have crushed you." Helen then checked in with Brianna the next day and reminded her, "You showed up. He didn't. He's the one who should be humiliated. As much as it hurts, it's better to know now what kind of guy he is. You deserve someone you can count on."

Helen was the voice of empathy and her daughter's encourager.

Though she missed doing "mom tasks" on a daily basis, Helen used her newly freed time to nurture her own life. She said yes more often to her husband's invitations to try a new restaurant, attend a fundraiser, or get away for the weekend. She increased her volunteer time with a beloved nonprofit. And she agreed to serve on several boards. All, of course, while maintaining consistent connection with Brianna, especially when her daughter needed her.

The relationship between Helen and Brianna did indeed become more friend-like over time. Brianna was reaching out to Helen more because she enjoyed talking to her mom. And Helen felt more like herself and not so "on the job" on those precious occasions she and Brianna got to hang out.

In the last few weeks of spring semester, Brianna called home in a panic. "Mom, I'm so upset. My friend Amy won't talk to me, and we were supposed to room together next year. There's no one I can room with. Everyone has a roommate but me. I'm freaking out!"

Mom knew Brianna was overwhelmed. She also knew this roommate issue was likely complicated by the pressure of exam week. Brianna tended to set sky-high expectations for herself, which further aggravated her ADHD and anxiety issues.

Helen was concerned for her daughter and tempted to fix the situation. But instead she said, "Why don't you go for a run and come up with four options of what you can do. Then write down the benefits and consequences of each choice. And call me back."

Brianna called her mom back in about an hour. They talked through her options, and Brianna figured out what her next step would be. Helen didn't fix her daughter's problem; that wasn't the goal. Rather, she equipped Brianna with the tools to solve her own problems.

And with that, Helen stepped fully into a new phase of parenting. Helen became the consultant.

As the consultant, Mom's role is one of a coach—not a fixer, and certainly not a monitor. As the consultant, you're there to encourage your daughter and provide advice—when asked—as she moves toward full-fledged adulthood.

Though the role of consultant might seem less intense from the outside than your previous parenting roles, it is no less critical. Make no mistake, there are going to be times your grown daughter will need you to speak into her life (remember the Maturity Gap), but now you'll be speaking as the consultant. And your counsel will serve to further develop and strengthen her ability to make mature decisions, implement effective problem-solving, and build her confidence in doing both.

To be effective as the consultant takes certain skills—like drawing and respecting boundaries, effective communication, and being strategic in how you offer guidance.

## "What's My Role?"

As the consultant, one of the toughest and most confusing questions you face is, "Whose business is it?" When your emerging adult is on shaky ground, you'll often find yourself asking, "What exactly is my role here?"

When we ask the question "What's my role?" what we're really asking is where the boundaries are. Some think of boundaries as barriers, a way of shutting people out. But boundaries actually allow for healthy relationships. And having a healthy relationship with your daughter is crucial to your being an effective consultant, as well as to furthering your enjoyment of this amazing person you've raised.

It's easy to fall into polarized thinking when it comes to boundaries. On the one hand, it seems right to put the responsibility for whatever has happened on your daughter. "She's an adult, she made her bed, now she should lie in it. How else will she learn?"

On the other hand, you worry that if she manages this situation poorly it could affect her future and maybe you should step in. So you hoist your daughter's burden on your shoulders, which both weighs you down and deprives her of the opportunity to solve her own problems and gain the self-confidence that brings with it.

Neither extreme is helpful. The truth of what skilled consulting requires is usually somewhere in the ambiguous middle.

The boundaries between parent and child have evolved and shifted over your daughter's life and will continue to do so. When she was little, her business was your business. You picked out her clothes, dressed her, changed her diaper, and made all her decisions for her. As she grew into adolescence, your daughter likely started challenging the lack of boundaries between you. And you probably let her negotiate a boundary or two. You let her make some choices for herself—like what her study habits would be or who to hang out with—so she could get a feel for handling her business. Still, until she graduated from high school, you—the monitor—reserved the right to revoke any boundary at will. Because as long as she was under your roof, her business was your business.

This disagreement over "business" boundaries is the root of much teen drama. Then, once our teens are out of the house, distance sets a natural boundary. As skilled consultants, we need to learn to work with that boundary and decide where to place or eliminate others.

## Her Business or Ours?

Just because your daughter is nearly grown doesn't mean you stop being a parent. It does, however, mean she has a life of her own that you don't have much say in. How she manages her life, who she sees, what she does are all, for the most part, no longer your business. They're hers. You can offer your well-earned wisdom, advice, and guidance, but what she does with it is no longer in your control.

However, if you've done a good job putting the five key facets in place, then you're likely to have built real trust between you, and she's likely to choose to seek and welcome your input, especially on bigger decisions—like how to spend the summer, where to live, who to date, and where to work. But ultimately, you, the consultant, have to respect that these things are now her business.

Note: There are times your daughter will want things to be your business when they're really her business. This tends to be around all things financial. If your daughter goes over her budget, she might look to you for more money. It's up to you to draw that boundary and make it clear that it's her business to manage her money.

Because boundaries are fluid and your daughter's move toward independence is a process, there remain areas of life where you two will continue to be connected for a time. This business should be considered *ours*—meaning both hers and yours.

For instance, if you're paying $50,000-plus a year on college tuition and your daughter is instead using it to get her PhD in partying, that's an *our business* situation. Again, your power is in your boundaries. You can tell your daughter she needs to go to class. But you can't make her. That's her part of this business. What you can decide, however, is to no longer invest your money in her tuition. That's your part of this business.

## Skillful Communication

Once you're clear on boundaries, the next step is upping your communication skills. As a mom—and a person who's lived in this world for more than a few decades—you have much wisdom to offer your daughter. But your offering counsel and her hearing it, let alone taking it, are very different things.

A skilled consultant sets the stage of openness, authenticity, and honesty (all things that the five key facets help you with). Both of you should feel free to express opinions and disagree respectfully. All communication should be two-way—where both of you feel heard and understood. And that starts with listening.

### Effective Listening

You know those times you try to talk to your daughter, and she's staring down at her phone saying "uh huh," and you know she's not listening? It's infuriating, right? Well, your daughter feels the same way if she thinks you're not hearing her. You may not be looking down at your phone, but many times our heads can be so full of what we're going to say there's no room to listen. We can't wait to stuff our advice down our daughter's throat like a mother bird feeding her chick. This is not effective listening.

Effective listening is both active and reflective. Active listening means you choose to be fully present with your daughter and really focus on what she's telling you, instead of what you want to tell her. You pay attention not only to what she says but also to her nonverbal cues. Is she struggling to find words? Does she seem uncomfortable? Do you feel she's holding something back? Is she her peppy self or does she seem lackluster?

Reflective listening is not only hearing what your daughter is saying but also listening with empathy and understanding. It's more than reflecting back word for word. It's reflecting back a more holistic picture.

Say your daughter tells you, "I hate online school. I'm sick of staring at a screen, and it's so hard to pay attention. At least if I were in class, I could talk to somebody."

You'd reflect back: "That makes sense to me. You've been doing this for months since the pandemic started. Your whole life has been disrupted. It's lonely staring at a screen. Of course, in-person school would be a ton better, especially seeing your friends every day."

Reflective listening communicates to your daughter that you care about what she's saying and want to understand, which makes her feel cared for and strengthens her trust in you. And because she knows you heard what she was saying, if you do have some advice, she's more likely to consider it.

Know that there will be times you reflect back and miss the mark. That's okay. Keep listening, your daughter will redirect you.

"Oh honey," you say, "I can understand you're feeling lonely."

"Mom, it's not that I'm lonely. I'm just having a really hard time paying attention, and that's freaking me out because I don't want to fall behind."

Also know that even when you don't quite capture your daughter's experience, she sees you trying, and that effort alone will bring you closer.

## The Art of Asking Questions

A key part of upping your communication game is knowing how to ask good questions. A skilled consultant knows all questions are not created equal. If you want an informative answer, you have to know how to phrase your question.

For instance, close-ended questions are good for gathering data points but not much else.

You: "How was your day?" Her: "Good."

You: "How did you test go?" Her: "Okay."

You: "Did you have a good weekend?" Her: "Yes."

You: "Did you have fun?" Her: "Yes."

They set you up for her one-word answers. And one-word answers shut down conversation. A skilled consultant uses open-ended questions whenever possible:

- "What do college kids do on the weekends these days?"
- "What do you like about Brendon?"
- "What's your English professor like?"
- "What do you think is going on with your roommate?"

This type of question gives your daughter the space to freely share what she wants without feeling pressured. It also allows you to get the information you want as well as information you didn't know you wanted. Open-ended questions lead to better conversations, fuller pictures of events, and therefore more understanding between you. For the skilled consultant, this type of question is the default.

Whenever possible, avoid the leading question. If not used carefully, this type of question can tick off your daughter. It can come off as judgmental—because it is. When you get right down to it, leading questions are judgmental statements with a question mark at the end.

- "You know you can't stay out until four in the morning and do well on your test the next day, right?"

- "You said you needed money last week and we gave you $200, but now you say there's no money?"

Attorneys are big fans of leading questions because they put their version of the truth in front of the jury before a witness has a chance to answer. If your daughter suspects you're trying to lead her, she'll shut down.

"Why" questions also come across as judgy, even if you don't mean them to be:

- "Why is it so hard to go to class?"
- "Why can't you get up in the morning?"

Such questions put your daughter on the defensive—not a good place for her to be if communication is your aim.

Whatever form of questions you choose, be careful not to bombard your daughter with them. "What are you doing this weekend? Where are you going? Who are you going with? When do you think you will work on your project?" When you throw out too many questions too fast—otherwise known as grilling—she's likely to think you're prying or trying to micromanage her. She'll think you have some sort of agenda, not that you're honestly interested. When you start a conversation with a hundred questions, she's not going to text you back or stay on the phone with you. And who can blame her?

## Be Strategic

Being the consultant doesn't come naturally to most moms. What's natural to us is to fix our daughters, overreact, panic, obsess, and take things personally. (I, myself, cop to all of this.) We get triggered into automatic responses because we love our daughters. We want them safe and happy. And if it's in our power to make that so, our brains tell us to do it. Just as we have for more than eighteen years.

But when you pause and break that down, emotional reactions are really about us and our instinctive need to ensure all is right in our child's world. To put it plainly, we are afraid. Triggers make us feel like we need to rush in and save our daughters. A skilled consultant resists this urge and takes time to sort through what her daughter needs right now. There's a good chance it's learning how to stand on her own two feet.

The best way we, as skilled consultants, can avoid giving in to our triggers is to have a strategy in place for handling triggering situations. I suggest to my clients (and I practice this myself) that whenever their daughters present them with a crisis, they take a breath, make a conscious choice to put their consultant hat on, and do the following four things before taking action.

## 1. Find the Right Time

Skilled consultants don't just jump in. They wait for the right time to explore the problem. If your daughter is upset, angry, and in the reactive part of her brain, she literally can't have a rational conversation or process your wonderful wisdom. If you, too, are in the reactive part of your brain, you're probably not seeing the situation clearly either.

So it's worth the wait until everyone is calm, until you won't be distracted or disturbed, until you know you'll have plenty of time. Then and only then will you and your daughter be in the right place to communicate well and find the best solution.

## 2. Gather Information

Let's say your daughter says, "I can't go to my classes today."

You automatically think and maybe even say, "Yes, you can. Go to class."

What you've done here is jumped to a conclusion and given advice before you've even tried to understand what's really going on. There could be a million reasons why she thinks she can't go to class:

- It could be because she stayed out until 4 a.m. and is hungover.

- It could be that she got in a fight with one of her friends, and she doesn't want to deal with seeing her in class.

- It could be that she didn't plan ahead and didn't know that her paper was due today.

- It could mean that her crush asked her to go skiing.

Skilled consultants make sure they have an accurate picture of a situation before dispensing advice. They get that picture by strategically gathering information. They get curious and let their curiosity open up a dialogue and direct the conversation. They might say,

- "Wow. I'm surprised. Tell me more."
- "What are the consequences of your taking that action?"
- "What made you think this way?"
- "What do your friends think about this? What do they think you should do?"

As their daughter talks, skilled consultants keep up an internal dialogue with questions like,

- *What's the story my daughter is telling herself?*
- *What has she tried or not tried?*
- *Has she thought it through?*
- *Does she have any solutions?*
- *What are the roadblocks or obstacles? Is this an internal obstacle, excuse, or story, or is this an external obstacle?*
- *Where is she stuck?*
- *Is my daughter not planning ahead and not having a long-term perspective?*
- *Is my daughter making rash decisions, using poor judgment, and not assessing risk?*
- *Is my daughter not controlling her impulses?*
- *Is my daughter letting her emotions run her life?*

Now I know, Mom, this takes patience. But remember your daughter needs a consultant because she is still neurologically immature. When you ask yourself these questions, evidence of that underdeveloped prefrontal cortex becomes evident. You can see your daughter's blind spots, so you get greater insight into what's really going on.

## 3. Clearly Identify the Problem

Using the information from your external and internal questioning, you then work to identify the problem. Knowing what the problem is makes it a whole lot easier to guide her in finding the right solution.

Let's say your questioning uncovered that your daughter skipped class because she didn't plan ahead and so didn't finish a paper that was due that day. This points you, the consultant, to her real issues here— time management, decision-making, and weighing consequences.

## 4. Be Relevant

One more caution as you enter this consultant role: whatever stories, encouragement, or advice you offer, make sure they're relevant to your daughter.

No matter how wise your wisdom is, for it to be useful, your daughter needs to see how it fits into her life and culture. If you start the conversation by saying, "Back when I was in college..." or "When you were a baby..." or "When I was a kid..." your daughter will tune you out. She doesn't see your experience "way back then" as relevant to her world today—though it very well may be. She'll also tune you out because she doesn't want to be you. She wants to be her unique self.

A skilled consultant keeps the questions, the conversations, and the counsel relevant to her daughter's culture, interests, and circumstances. Keep it relevant, and your daughter will lean in and listen.

The exception to this is in matters of the heart. Your experience here is always relevant because you're sharing your vulnerability. Examples of this are: How you felt when you made a D in statistics. When your boyfriend cheated on you. When you knew you were in love. Knowing you experienced the same feelings, heartbreaks, and firsts and went on to live a full and happy life will help your daughter put her own highs and lows in perspective. She'll know she can be resilient like her mother.

## The Skilled Consultant in Action

As a skilled consultant, your goal is not to get your daughter to follow your advice (no matter how spot-on it is). Your goal is to guide your daughter into thinking for herself and finding her own solutions— to get her to exercise that underdeveloped PFC and get those neural pathways in shape.

My client Jada did this masterfully with her daughter, Jasmine. During a session with me, Jada explained that Jasmine, a sophomore in college, was living for the first time in an apartment. She'd given Jasmine plenty of money for food at the first of the month. Yet, halfway through the month, Jasmine called home crying, "I have no money and no food. Send me more money." Jada said, "I can't believe I raised such a privileged girl."

I suggested to Jada that maybe it's not that Jasmine is so privileged but that she's on a learning curve. Maybe she needs to learn to budget. Last year, Jasmine didn't have to worry about food because she was on the dorm's meal plan. This made sense to Jada.

So, I coached her in how to be a skilled consultant—how to communicate, ask probing questions, and identify the problem. And then how to choose the right time to guide her daughter to think for herself.

When it was time to communicate with Jasmine, Jada asked her daughter those open-ended questions, like where she bought food. She found out that Jasmine shopped at Whole Foods and habitually ordered from Grubhub.

With a tone of curiosity (not judgment), Jada asked (not advised) Jasmine if she'd visited other grocery stores and checked their prices. She also asked Jasmine if she was aware of how much money she spent on Grubhub. I know this sounds like common sense. But these practical questions were teaching Jasmine how to think about her spending.

Finally, Jada said, "Honey, I don't think you have a money problem, I think you just need to learn to budget. What do you think?"

Jasmine agreed and asked her mom to show her how. She also asked for simple recipes she could cook on the weekend and eat during the week. "That will help me avoid Grubhub," Jasmine said. "Yes, it will," Jada replied, proud of her daughter for thinking of that.

Jada didn't get a phone call the next month. Jasmine stuck to her food budget. But most important, this mother didn't solve her daughter's problem. She taught her how to think things through and offered wisdom and support when asked.

Renee's daughter, Brook, was a junior in college when she met Gavin, the man of her dreams. They'd been dating for eight months.

Renee loved Gavin. He treated Brook with respect. He had career goals. She could tell how happy they were together. This was a huge relief for Renee, especially since Brook's previous boyfriend, Chad, had cheated on her and was abusive.

Renee told me that in the middle of a conversation one day, Brook said, "Remember David?"

"Yes," Renee said. David was rich and good looking. He'd wined and dined Brook at the most expensive restaurant in town. They'd gone out for a few months, but nothing serious. They'd both dated other people at the same time.

"He called me and asked me to go to this amazing place for dinner, and I said yes."

Renee thought, *What are you thinking?* But instead, she asked, "Does Gavin know?"

"No," Brook replied.

"Hmmm," Renee paused. "How would you feel if Gavin took a girl out to the most expensive restaurant in town even though they were 'just friends'?"

"I'd be furious at him," said Brook. And then she paused. "Oh, why am I sabotaging myself?"

"Good question. Do you know?"

"Mom, I think I'm freaked out because I reached out to Gavin, and he didn't answer his phone, and he always answers his phone, so I got scared he was cheating on me. When David asked me to dinner, I probably said yes to get back at Gavin."

"What are you going to do now?" asked Renee.

"I'm not going to go, of course."

By being a skilled consultant, Renee helped Brook slow down her thinking, gain some insight, weigh some consequences, and make a better decision.

In both these cases, the moms didn't tell their daughters what to think or what to do. Both gently guided them to see their situation more fully, and then trusted these young women to draw good conclusions and take smart actions.

## The Benefits of Being a Consultant

This consultant phase of parenting isn't a time of growth for only your daughter; it's a time of growth for your mother-daughter relationship and for you too.

In the business world, people leave their companies and become consultants because they're tired of being in the thick of things and having to maneuver office politics day in, day out. As consultants, they're still involved with their companies, and they still help to guide them. But they're not in the office, so they don't get drawn into the office drama.

Consultant-moms enjoy those same benefits. You're still involved and called in when advice is needed. But because your daughter is no longer in your home, you're out of the daily drama and being in the thick of things with her. With the physical distance comes less worry and agony. All that freed attention opens more space in your life to do what you want.

Your daughter, too, is experiencing freedom from you. She needs this freedom to be able to grow up—make her choices, deal with her successes, and clean up after her failures. It's in this stumbling forward toward adulthood that she discovers who she is and how she wants to live her life.

In high school, my daughter had a very messy room (I'm sure you can relate). Worse, she'd leave her things scattered around the house. To be honest, I anticipated my daughter would always have a messy home. But recently, her grown-up sensibilities blew me away: During a visit to my house, she asked if I could pick up several Mr. Clean Magic Eraser Sponges for her while I was out because she wanted to clean the kitchen. *My kitchen* was driving *her* crazy! Point being, you just never know.

The consultant walks the tightrope between giving her daughter the freedom and space to discover who she is while staying connected and speaking into her life. It's a challenge, to be sure. But it's one that's well worth the effort because it's how you preserve and grow your relationship. Consulting does get easier with time and practice.

As your daughter stands on the brink of adulthood, the best thing you can do for her (and you) is put your relationship above any personal agenda you have for her. You might want her to stay in college and enter a profession. But she might choose to quit school and become a singer-songwriter or work at a ski resort for a season or hike the Appalachian Trail. You can consult, you can help her to think these choices through, but in the end, the best thing you can do is support her. Let her know that wherever she goes in this world and whatever she does, you love her and are there for her always.

Though seemingly paradoxical, you and your daughter giving each other the freedom to find your own way will bring you closer together. As the years go on and she matures, the strong, dependable relationship you've nurtured through this transitional time will bring you both amazing joy and carry you through any messy, hard, or challenging times ahead.

## Exercise: The Consultant's Reward

SIT BACK. Close your eyes. And imagine meeting your daughter in your favorite spot five years from now.

1  Think about her...

- What has she accomplished thus far in life?
- What dreams is she working toward?
- Where does she live, what does she like, and who are the people who populate her life?

2  Think about you...

- What have you done in the last five years?
- What's on your agenda for the next five?
- Who populates your life now?

3   Think about your mother-daughter relationship...

- How is it different from what it was five years ago?
- How has your role changed? How has her role changed?
- What will it look like in another five years?

If you wish, write out your answers. Seal them in an envelope and put the envelope someplace safe. Make a date with yourself to open the envelope in five years and read what you wrote—maybe even share it with your daughter.

# 6

# Setbacks

---

**H**ELEN AND BRIANNA enjoyed a rich relationship throughout Brianna's freshman and sophomore years at SMU. There were a few of the usual bumps in the road, but Helen, now firmly established in her consultant role, successfully helped her daughter learn to navigate them.

As Brianna headed off for her junior year, Helen's heart was full. She couldn't believe Brianna was halfway through college already. She was so proud of her daughter's progress. Brianna was right on track.

But not two months into the new semester, Helen sensed something was wrong. Having stayed in regular contact with Brianna, Helen was well aware that her daughter was struggling with her coursework. But this seemed to be more than that. In the last couple of weeks, when Helen texted something silly, Brianna's replies hadn't been as playful as usual. And twice, when Helen called in the middle of the day, Brianna was still in bed. This was not like Brianna. Her normal reaction to stress was to go into overdrive.

So when Brianna's roommate called to say she was worried because Brianna wasn't eating, wouldn't get out of bed, hadn't been to class, and had talked about suicide—Helen didn't hesitate to act. Whatever was going on, Helen knew it was beyond Brianna's current ability to manage. Helen made the command decision to break previously set boundaries, step up to the frontlines, and take charge. A good consultant knows when to triage.

Within seconds of hanging up the phone, Helen jumped in the car and headed to SMU, where she found what looked like a severely depressed Brianna. She packed up her daughter, brought her home, and called me for an emergency appointment. A good consultant also knows when to refer.

Just a note here: This situation is the perfect illustration as to why it is so important to put those five key facets into practice and make the move from monitor to consultant once your daughter is out from under your roof. It was thanks to Helen's staying in touch with Brianna—and Brianna welcoming that contact—that Helen was aware that something more than the usual was wrong and knew to take the roommate's concerns seriously. Also, because the roommate had witnessed the quality of this mother-daughter relationship, she felt comfortable calling her roommate's mom with her concerns.

When I met with Helen and Brianna, Brianna shared that she'd not only thought about suicide, she had a detailed plan. I agreed she was suffering a major depression and suggested she meet immediately with a psychiatrist for a firm diagnosis and any necessary medication, and then continue regular therapy with me. With her mom looking on, Brianna came to the decision that it might be best to take a semester off. We all agreed.

Once the immediate crisis passed and Brianna was in the hands of professionals, working toward recovery, Helen stepped back from the frontlines and returned to her role as her daughter's consultant—still right there and ready if Brianna needed her.

## The Significant Setback

When we send our daughters off to college, we all imagine they'll love their roommates. They'll have a great group of friends, and when they go out, they'll have good clean fun. They'll get into the sorority of their choice. They'll do well in their classes. They'll start dating the perfect person. They'll get an amazing internship, graduate in four years, snare their dream job, move into the perfect apartment, and be financially independent. In that order.

When our daughters first leave, we have lots of hope and also lots of fear. Eventually, we let the fear go (or get used to it) and are able to engage in our own life. Then we get the call. And what she has to tell us isn't her usual boyfriend drama or dented car or send-money issue. It's more significant than that—a serious accident, a consequential failure, a grave mistake, an illness, a crime against her. Significant enough to change her life.

This significant setback hits us like a lightning bolt through our nervous system. The glide path we thought our child was on has hit turbulence, bad—upending our expectations and crashing our daughter's life into uncertainty. We worry for her future. We want nothing more than to jump in and put her back on that certain path. That's a natural reaction for a parent, but, unfortunately, not one grounded in reality.

## Perfect Progress Versus Imperfect Progress

Though Helen was standing strong for Brianna on the outside, on the inside she was concerned that this depression was a significant setback for her daughter. Everything had been going so well. Brianna was on schedule to graduate "on time." Of course, Brianna's health came first. But still, Helen couldn't help but worry that missing fall exams and then taking off the entire spring would put Brianna a year "behind."

When Helen brought her concerns to me privately, I asked, "A year behind what?"

We're programmed by movies, media, magazines, and our mothers to believe that there's an ideal progression from high school graduation to adulthood. We want this ideal for our daughters with all our hearts, so anything short of this feels like a big cosmic disappointment. What's underneath this Hallmark version of college life and beyond, however, is the dangerous and ridiculous premise of "perfect" progress.

Of course, it's important for the young adult to see they're making progress in life. It boosts their self-esteem and motivation. It keeps despair at bay. The problem comes when our cultural propensity for perfectionism—all-or-nothing thinking—creeps into their vision and their expectations for themselves.

Perfectionism is a mean game. It demands everything, and yet it's impossible to win because life doesn't work that way. Perfect progress on a graph looks like a straight arrow toward success. It implies you must have continuous forward motion in every single area of your life at the same time. By that standard, let's say your daughter works hard and makes great progress in one area—like she aced her organic chemistry project. On the very same day, she ate one too many tacos and fell off the healthy-eating wagon. Off goes the buzzer, and she's a loser in the perfect-progress game of life.

This makes perfectionism a dangerous game as well. Not being able to acknowledge and celebrate each success as it comes—no matter what's happening in the rest of her life—keeps her from realizing she's progressing at all and opens the door to despair.

Perfectionism and pressure go hand in hand—especially for young women—stealing their joy, creativity, innovation, peace, hope. Feeling this pressure, young people often either push themselves to exhaustion or worse, thinking they're not good enough (as Brianna did), or they become so afraid of failure that they lower their goals, stop trying new things, and lose their motivation.

Perfect progress is a lie. There's no ideal path to adulthood or set timeline to get there. Each person matures in their own way. Brianna's setback and the consequences of it are just as much a part of who she is, her story, her timeline for growth, as her first steps, her high school graduation, and her acceptance to SMU.

When we wake up out of the fantasy fog of perfect progress, we realize that real progress—real human development—is jagged, messy, and unpredictable. This is especially true for young adults finding their way in the world. Not to mention that what we call mistakes—veering off our perfect-progress trajectory—are typically where the most valuable life-learning occurs. A setback, even a significant one, is not the end of the road. It's a detour. And there are many gifts to be gained off the beaten path.

It's better for your daughter's mental health, more beneficial to her progress, and better for you, Mom, to set the expectation at what I like to call imperfect progress. As you know, your daughter's neurologically immature brain is wired for poor decisions and mistakes at this point in her life. Imperfect progress is realistic, normal, and doable.

As your daughter strikes out in the world, she—like all of us—will make progress in some areas of life while she struggles in others. After all, issues she grappled with in high school—self-esteem, relationships, partying, time management, anxiety, procrastination, and the like—go with her when she moves to college. It's only rational to expect some trial and error (imperfect progress) as she learns to manage these problem areas for herself. Sometimes her progress will look more like three steps forward and two steps back. And that's okay.

Because when the expectation is set at imperfect progress, she's free of shame and fear of failure. She can give herself full credit and celebrate when she succeeds in one area, while at the same time she is still working on another. This continuous recognition of her progress, however it occurs, is what strengthens her motivation, makes her resilient, and allows her to grow in her own time into a fully realized and mature adult.

I'm sure there were a few unexpected detours on your road to adulthood. I know I had a few. That's because setbacks are part of adult life. Each one may feel like the end of her world, but you know from your own experience they're not. Your job now is to make sure your daughter knows that too.

When a setback occurs, you, Mom (as no one else can), must hold space for both your daughter's genius as well as her failing. When she's lost faith in herself, you must help her to be realistic about what's happened but also know she has the strength to get through it. You don't need to lecture her. She's already being pulled down into the dark hole of despair. She doesn't need you to point that out. Your job is to remind her of who she is, of her progress thus far in life, and of how big her light truly is. She needs to know you believe in her. She needs you to give her hope.

## This Setback Does Not Belong to You

To hold that space for her means to fully recognize that it's her setback, not yours, even though it sure can feel like it's happening to you. Like it's your dream that's been lost. That's because part of this is true; you have a dream for your daughter, which never includes seeing her suffering, struggling, or stalling out. And, Mom, if we're being honest here, part of us wants her to be successful so we can tell our friends of her accomplishments.

When a significant setback happens, you need to be aware of whatever story you're telling yourself, and then acknowledge and process your disappointments head-on. If you don't, it can get messy. Whatever strong emotions you're feeling—disappointment, grief, sadness, anxiety, hopelessness, anger, criticism, judgment, frustration—can come directly or sideways at your daughter. She'll pick up on your energy and attitude in a second and react to them—taking the focus off handling her setback. So deal with your own heart first.

I strongly recommend you journal what's coming up for you. If it's a feeling like sadness, ask yourself, "Why am I so sad?" Maybe you think, *Who'll want to marry my daughter when she's been raped?* If so, you then ask what's the feeling under that thought. Perhaps it's sadness or despair.

Now ask yourself if what you think is really true. Is her life over? Will really no one marry her if she's been raped? No, obviously, that's not true. So, what is true? "My daughter has trauma from the rape and needs help. My daughter needs me to be there for her and hold hope that she can get past it."

How you show up for your daughter matters immensely to her managing this setback well and to your relationship. If you're having trouble getting past strong thoughts and feelings, contact a therapist and work through your feelings so you can be present for your daughter. You don't want her to be taking care of you. You certainly don't want to make her setback worse.

When my daughter was six months old, her dad had an affair. I will spare you the details, but we ultimately got divorced. It was not what I wanted. I felt like such a failure, especially considering I was a marriage and family therapist and had been full-time youth minister too. It was very public. I felt a lot of shame.

My mom is a staunch Catholic and a force of nature. I was concerned about how she would react because the Catholic Church is not big on divorce. But when I told my mom, she immediately took my side and didn't make it about her (or her religion). She let me know she believed me and believed in me. She was my champion through these uncharted and unwanted waters. She was one of my shining stars that guided me in a very dark night. I'll never forget how she stood by me and supported me. The silver lining in that terrible time in my life is it brought my mom and me closer.

So, when your daughter comes to you with a significant setback, don't mix in your stuff. Lay aside the judgment and criticism. Deal with your issues on your own. Because your daughter needs you to be one of her shining stars.

## Dealing With the Dirt

After a significant setback, your daughter is vulnerable. She's most likely struggling with her confidence, her emotions, her decisions, her relationships, and what to do next. Not surprisingly, this can overwhelm her and send her into the stress response of fight, flight, or freeze.

You'll know she's in *fight* if she lashes out, blames, and becomes angry at the world because of her setback. "I hate my professors. They're all idiots. 'F' *them* for failing me." You'll know she's in *flight* if she ignores or avoids her setback or literally takes off for parts unknown. "Mom, I'm going to go to Thailand for three months." And you'll know she's in *freeze* if she does nothing and is unable to move forward. Which is what happened to Brianna. She became so stressed by her coursework that she froze, which exacerbated other problem areas in her life. One thing piled on the next, leaving her susceptible to a full-blown depression.

As your daughter's shining star, part of your job is to keep a light on the reality of her setback for her so she can deal with the issues that led to the significant setback and the fallout from it and find the right path forward. This journey is likely to be painful before it gets hopeful.

But take heart, Mom. Think of this analogy. When you plant a seed in the ground the first thing that comes up is dirt, not the new seedling—and definitely not the fruit or the flowers. So, when you see the dirt—the setback and the struggle—it's evidence of your daughter's impending growth. Just underneath that dirt is the new seedling. If there was no seedling under there ready and wanting to burst forth, there would be no dirt coming up. Digging her way out of the setback clears the dirt and makes room for her growth.

But the dirt does hurt. Shame, denial, fear, and admitting she needs help all might come up as she digs. She might become resistant or may try to avoid the dig by making more bad choices—like drinking, drugs, or, like Brianna, not reaching out for help soon enough. As her shining star, you can guide her away from avoidance and encourage her to keep digging by letting her know you are there for her and she's up to the task.

Often, we see evidence of dirt coming up without knowing what's really underneath it. Your daughter's not doing well in school. She's isolating from you or her friends. You can tell that she's not happy. You see a sudden change in her personality or who she hangs out with. She can't focus. She seems all over the place. She's edgy on the phone.

Here, I'm going to ask you to do a very hard thing: Don't overreact, but also don't minimize the dirt. You need to stay present to what's showing up and be curious. Avoid all labeling or judging—like my daughter is "lazy" or "easy." There may be something deeper going on. You want to create that safe place where your daughter can talk to you.

Helping your daughter move the dirt so the seedling can make itself known and thrive starts with your asking three questions:

1   What needs to heal?
2   What issues need to be addressed?
3   What is the best next step?

## What Needs to Heal?

Many mental health issues that were well under control while your daughter lived at home can reappear and worsen when your daughter is learning to manage on her own. This could be anxiety, depression, self-harm, eating disorders, or any issues from past trauma like sexual assault, loss, grief, or abandonment.

Your role here is not to try to be your daughter's counselor, but to be her consultant. It's not all on your shoulders, thank God! But often, because you're so intimately familiar with your daughter, you're positioned better than anyone else to know what's causing her setback and thus what needs to heal.

Barbara, a pediatrician, drove up to see her daughter, Maryanne, a sophomore in college. She hadn't seen Maryanne in six weeks and so noticed right away that her daughter had dropped twenty pounds. To Barbara, she looked emaciated.

While her friends were asking Maryanne how she did it and telling her how good she looked, Barbara knew there was a problem. This drastic weight loss coupled with Maryanne's recent complaining about her roommates, her classes, and not having enough time to herself told Barbara that the eating disorder Maryanne had suffered in high school had returned. Barbara picked up the phone and asked me to start working with Maryanne before this turned into a life-threatening situation.

What Barbara saw—an escalating eating disorder—wasn't apparent to anyone else. Maryanne had exhibited these tendencies in high school, but at home, under her mother's watchful eye, the issue had been managed. What Barbara knew from that time was there was a deeper issue that wasn't about food. It had to do with anxiety. The more anxious Maryanne got, the more pressure she put on herself to be perfect, the more she struggled with an eating disorder. Barbara knew what needed to be healed here was Maryanne's anxiety.

Over time, with a lot of digging in some painful dirt, and her mom there to support her all the way, Maryanne learned to manage her anxiety herself and let go of her restrictive behaviors around food. She has a plan for what to do when she becomes anxious. She also has a plan for how to reach out for help if her anxiety becomes too much to handle alone. Today, thanks to this significant setback forcing her to get the help she needed, she's a much happier person, enjoys having friends, has graduated from college, and is headed to medical school.

## What Issues Need to Be Addressed?

Sometimes it's not something that needs to be healed that causes or is caused by the setback, but something that needs to be faced, to be dealt with—such as alcohol or drug abuse, gender or sexual identity, learning disorders, self-management, loneliness, or anger management. As a mother, you're at the greatest advantage to help your daughter uncover this issue or to refer her to a therapist who can.

Anne was at a loss as to why her daughter Makayla, a freshman in her spring semester, wouldn't get out of bed and go to class. So she made an appointment for Makayla with both me and a psychiatrist. (Often it takes a team.)

At my first session with Anne and Makayla, Makayla shared that she'd been sick with mononucleosis over Thanksgiving, and it had taken six weeks to recover. She went back to school in January then fell sick with the flu in February.

When I talked with Makayla alone, she told me she's by herself a lot at school and feels she missed out on so much when she was sick. I responded that it must have been hard to be in bed while her roommate was going out. She nodded her head sheepishly. I could tell that wasn't the issue.

She started our third session by telling me how ashamed she was and that she worried that people thought she was terrible. I was confused. "About being sick?" I asked. "No," she said, and explained that for three months prior to getting mono, she was going out four nights a week. She'd pledged a sorority and frequently partied at several fraternity houses. Anxious being around boys, she started drinking and would continue until she'd pass out. More than once, she woke up in a boy's room. At first, her behavior surprised her. But then hooking up with several guys in one night became normal. She told me the worst night was when she'd gone on a date to a party with one guy and woke up the next morning with another.

She was feeling humiliated by her behavior. That, along with not feeling well, became one of the reasons she didn't want to go to class. She also felt she'd earned a bad reputation. Then she told me she'd never have acted this way when she was sober.

Makayla's issue was social anxiety complicated by alcohol abuse. Alcoholism ran in her family, so in addition to therapy for the social anxiety, I encouraged Makayla to attend Alcoholics Anonymous meetings, which she did. Because of Covid-19, Makayla had to stay home the rest of the semester, which allowed her to stay out of the party scene and get her life back on track. She worked out every day and caught up with her classwork. She started smiling again, and I could see the real, vibrant Makayla.

If you're not sure what the actual issue is, that's okay. Start with what you see, like Anne did. If your daughter's life is unraveling in any way, tell her you're sorry that she's having a bad time, state what you see as the issue, and then put the idea of talking with a therapist on the table. You might say something like, "I'm so sorry your girlfriend broke up with you. It seems like there's a lot going on in your relationship. This could be a good time to sort things out with a therapist." If you think you know what the real issue is, you can say something like, "It seems from what you just shared you could benefit with someone helping you with organization or self-management."

Then you can connect her with a good doctor, psychotherapist, or coach—whatever is needed. Let them be the one to evaluate her. Again, she doesn't need a lecture or advice from you. You're the skilled consultant helping her triage support, resources, and services. (By the way, a good place to access academic, medical, and psychological services is at her university.)

## What Is the Best Next Step?

Once you've identified what needs to heal and what issue or issues need to be dealt with, you'll want to think about the best next step for your daughter. Often—like for Brianna, Maryanne, and Makayla—this is booking a therapy appointment. But it can be connecting your daughter to any resource to help her heal and work toward recovery.

The "best next step" should always be a healing step—never a punishment from you "to teach her a lesson," which is really being harsh and reactive. "I'm taking away your car," "I'm not paying for college," "Find another place to live; I'm not paying your rent"—that's you trying to wrest control of a situation that's well out of your control. Besides, if the significant setback was due to her negligence or poor decision-making, the natural consequences are likely punishment enough. She'll learn her lesson through the pain of what's she's lost, who she's hurt, and having to implement whatever remedy she can. Most likely, she already feels bad. Punishment imposed by you doesn't motivate; it undermines her growing sense of responsibility and only damages your relationship.

The skilled consultant waits until she is calm and clear. She sets boundaries and gives consequences always with the intention of helping her daughter heal and mature. Here are some questions to ask yourself to help you think through the best next step:

- What will build my daughter's confidence, develop her gifts, get her curious about a career, and broaden her experiences?

- What will help her build healthy relationships and find a place to belong? What will help her grow in responsibility with herself and others?

- What will help her grow in maturity and become a healthy, connected, and independent adult?

- What will stretch (not terrify) her and get her out of her comfort zone?

- What is the fastest way my daughter can experience a success and see she's making progress?

Helping your daughter find and take her "best next step" will allow her to see she can make progress, even after a significant setback. Seeing progress will motivate her to push that dirt away, so she can see the sprout and give it all the sun it needs to flourish.

## Think Outside the College Box

When you're considering the best next step, consider that getting a college degree does not equal independence. Many young people graduate from college, can't get a job, and move back home. It's not the end of your daughter's world if she doesn't get a college degree right now, or ever.

Though I have three master's degrees, college was not the direction my daughter chose. She's a kinesthetic learner. After high school, she decided to earn an advanced certification in massage. Then she added certification in yoga instruction, Ayurvedic counseling, and meditation instruction—and opened her own business. Today, she's a self-supporting entrepreneur who loves what she does. She's works on professional athletes, celebrities, and MDs who tell her that she gave them the best massage they've ever had.

I would encourage you to stay open to new paths and experiences—especially after a significant setback. Maybe your daughter needs to take a semester off or transfer to another school. Maybe your daughter could take a gap year, get professional certification, or get an internship or job to learn about a career she's interested in. The key here is you want a best next step your daughter is excited about and is doable for her.

## When Bad Things Happen

Nothing causes us more suffering than when bad things happen to our daughters. I've worked with girls who had to take a semester off college because they'd been raped. Even when the bad thing is not as abhorrent or trauma-inducing as an assault, it can still knock the wind out of our girls, and us.

Whatever happens, we need to be strong for our daughters. If they think they can't come to us because we're going to fall apart, they'll try to handle it on their own, which often means ignoring it. That's not what we want or what they need. They need our support and mature prefrontal cortex to give them guidance as they put themselves back together.

My daughter attended a high school for performing arts and specialized in dance. By the time she was a junior, she'd had two knee injuries and back injury. At nineteen, she decided she wanted to help other athletes who'd suffered injuries—that's how she chose massage. When she was two-thirds through her certification courses, specializing in sports massage, another student worked on her during practicum and reinjured my daughter's back. My daughter's right arm froze up. She couldn't bend or move it.

We went to the emergency room. An inexperienced resident didn't listen to what my daughter told them about her injury and yanked her arm back and forth. This damaged the serratus anterior muscle, which destabilized my daughter's scapula. In January 2015, my daughter had major surgery on her back and arm—and wouldn't be able to use that arm for the next nine months to a year.

It was so hard to see my daughter go through this. This was a significant setback. My daughter couldn't complete her massage certification. And she couldn't find a job where she didn't need her right arm (she's right-handed). My daughter was angry, sad, and devastated. It was hard not being pulled into her despair. I had to go deep into my own faith to be her anchor. And yes, I turned to my own support group to hold me up during this time.

As awful as it was and as heartbroken as I was for my daughter, I also got to watch her mature over the year it took for her arm to heal. She stepped up and took responsibility for her healing by going to the gym religiously to strengthen the muscles in her arm and back—without my nagging or scheduling or overseeing her workouts. Two years after the surgery, of her own volition, she went back to school and got that massage certification—and you know the rest.

Often a significant setback can feel like everything's over and that your daughter (and you) will never recover. But that's not true. A setback is never the end of the story; ask any mom of a young adult. In fact, I encourage you to do just that. They can help you to know that these setbacks—while gut-wrenching in the moment—can be the catalyst that helps your daughter heal old wounds so she can grow up and grow into an even more responsible and compassionate adult.

## Exercise: The Progress Journal

FOLLOW THESE STEPS to embrace the gifts of imperfect progress:

1 Write down one situation that exemplifies your daughter's moving forward in life. Examples: She got a good grade. She wrote her paper before it was due. She did her laundry before coming home.

2 Write down an area in which your daughter is struggling. Examples: She overslept and missed her 8 a.m. class again. She complains about the way her boyfriend treats her but doesn't break up with him. She forgot to study for a test.

3 Write down where you've seen progress—even small progress—in that struggle. Example: She put all her scheduled tests on her calendar with an alert for the day before so she'd know to set her alarm.

4 Next time you talk with her, choose some items where she's made obvious progress and congratulate her. Choose one item from the progress list and least one item from the struggle file to let her know you see her trying.

5 If the timing feels right, tell her about one of your own struggles. Use the opportunity to remind her that the expectation is imperfect progress and mistakes are how we learn.

# 7

# Healing Conversations

CAROLYN AND DAVID had been married for twenty-eight years. David provided well for the family, and Carolyn was a stay-at-home mom. They had two young adult daughters, Alexis and Hannah.

Alexis, the older of the two, had been an easy kid and a hard worker. She'd taken all honors classes in high school, lettered in sports, and graduated third in her class. Emotionally even-keeled, she'd always had a solid group of friends. After high school, she went straight to college and was now in graduate school at Vanderbilt.

Hannah didn't fit as neatly into the world as her sister. She did fine in school but was nowhere near the top of her class. She was more into theater and music than sports. Her friends were on the fringy side but always interesting and nice. People constantly compared Hannah to her sister, which made Hannah feel less than. Deep down, she grew up suspecting even her parents liked Alexis better.

One night when Hannah was a junior in high school, she left a party, went speeding down the street, lost control, and hit a tree. Miraculously, she was okay, but the car was totaled. The police were called to the scene, gave her a breathalyzer, and arrested her for driving under the influence. Hannah spent the night in a holding cell. When her parents came to get her the next morning, the look of sadness and disappointment on their faces just added to Hannah's humiliation. Though her parents tried to help her work through what happened, learn from the experience, and move on with her life, Hannah never forgave herself for being so stupid.

After high school graduation, Hannah didn't think she was ready for a four-year school, so she chose to go to a community college two hours from home. When she had a less than stellar spring semester in her second year, her parents suggested she take a break from school to think about next steps. She agreed, moved back in with them, and got a job as a hostess at a nearby chain restaurant.

On one of Hannah's days off, Carolyn treated her to a day of shopping. They bought Hannah new clothes, had the brakes fixed on her car, and had lunch at Hannah's favorite café. Carolyn felt they'd had a wonderful day together and was so happy to have had this one-on-one time with her younger daughter.

Once home and in the kitchen getting ready to make dinner, Carolyn asked Hannah, who was twenty, if she wanted a glass of wine.

"What's with you people?" Hannah snapped at her mother out of nowhere. "You want to know why I got a DUI in high school? You're always pushing the alcohol. You gave me martinis when I was in tenth grade. Every holiday and birthday, we had to have peach Bellinis, Bloody Marys, or a pitcher of margaritas. You and dad drink a bottle of wine every night. You're alcoholics."

Carolyn was stunned by this outburst and went straight into defensive mode. "After everything I've done for you today, that's how you speak to me? Your daddy and I are not alcoholics. How dare you judge us! Your daddy has provided you everything you need."

"Just say it, Mom. I know you're thinking it," Hannah shot back. *"What does Hannah know? She can't even make it through community college. Alexis wouldn't talk like that.* Well, maybe you're right. Maybe Alexis wouldn't. But the truth is the truth."

With that, the conversation stopped. They were at a stalemate.

Carolyn, now crying, felt confused. Where had this come from? Hadn't they just spent a delightful day together taking care of

Hannah's every need? Hadn't she just spent a fortune on clothes and getting her daughter's car fixed?

Carolyn also felt guilty. Alcohol did flow freely in their home. And truth be told, while she loved her girls equally, Alexis was predictable and a lot easier to be around. She appreciated Hannah's idiosyncrasies, but they also worried her.

That was the adult reality of the situation. So, Hannah wasn't totally wrong. But she wasn't totally right either. The situation was more nuanced and reasoned than Hannah's not-yet-adult brain could understand. But Carolyn's defensive tactics left no room for her to bring Hannah to that more mature understanding—and eventual healing. Instead, both mom and daughter retreated to their corners with their own truths and their own hard feelings.

Carolyn called me the next day, still shaken. When we met, I explained to her that such exchanges are normal between moms and young adult daughters and to be prepared for more of these outbursts. Then over several sessions, I coached her how to turn these hard conversations into healing conversations that would help Hannah mature and ultimately bring mother and daughter closer.

## The Hard (Hurtful) Conversation

We all experience hard conversations as we go through life. Usually, they begin with words like "we need to talk" or "sit down." But the type of conversation I'm talking about here—between mother and emerging-adult daughter—typically just explode into the air, seemingly out of nowhere, catching you off guard and emotionally unprepared for the assault.

You're putzing around the house, watching TV together, or driving with your daughter to the grocery store. Then all of a sudden, she's shouting at you, accusing you of bad parenting, not loving her enough, or doing her some wrong in childhood:

"You never cooked for me when I was growing up, all you gave me was frozen dinners."

"You never made time for me."

"Did you even consider how I'd feel when you divorced Dad? My whole life was turned upside down, and you didn't care."

"Why did we have to move my junior year? You made me leave all my friends. You ruined my senior year."

As hard as it is to believe, these outbursts are not really about *you.* They're about *her.* It's likely your daughter has been talking to her boyfriend or roommate or is just trying to make sense of her own life. She starts digging through the dirt (the issues) in her life and triggers some intense feelings, such as anger or sadness. Because she hasn't yet developed the neural connections to think through the emotion and neutralize this energy herself, she defuses her overwhelm by lashing out at you. You become her go-to when she's in pain. More than likely, she's not consciously aware of what's really going on.

Needless to say, your daughter's blaming, judging, and accusing you of ruining her life makes this a hard conversation. It's incredibly painful for moms.

However, when you merely react to her attack out of your own hurt, it can build a wall of distrust that can last a lifetime. I once counseled a sixty-five-year-old daughter who didn't want to deal with her ninety-year-old mom. The mom desperately needed her daughter's help, but the daughter didn't want to engage because of hurt feelings from her twenties.

Navigating through a hard conversation is like being Indiana Jones entering the Temple of Doom, going after the mystical stone. The treasure you're after is your daughter's healing and strengthening your relationship. The goal is to transform the hard conversation into a healing conversation.

## Why Is She Doing This?

The dirt that surfaces in your daughter comes from the wounds and traumas of her childhood. That dirt stokes her current struggles and actively interferes with her ability to maturely think through and manage issues—around perfection, body image, self-confidence, and relationships—in her present life.

Some of your daughter's trauma is the result of life being hard: Your husband died suddenly when your daughter was nine. You had breast cancer. Her sibling had serious health problems as she was growing up. Her uncle killed himself. Your house flooded or burned down. Your husband lost his job.

Some of her trauma does stem from life decisions and arguably some mistakes you made as a parent that were—and perhaps still are—beyond her level of experience and understanding: Your divorcing her father because he was not a partner to you. Your taking a promotion because it meant more money, but which also meant you weren't always home for dinner. Your not paying for the private college she wanted because state college was absolutely fine and she'd graduate without debt.

While it was super hard for you maneuvering through these tragedies and through your life, these twists and turns also impacted your daughter. Children don't have the capacity to process big tragedies or changes wholly in the moment, and so they often experience delayed reactions in their twenties.

Also, though she's physically fully grown, your daughter doesn't yet see you as a mere mortal. She likely still regards you as Wonder Woman—almighty, infallible, and high on your pedestal. The person who can soothe her, protect her, and meet all her needs—just as you did when she was a child.

So, when her twenty-something brain is processing an old trauma or wound, it questions why Wonder Woman didn't come to her rescue. She believes you had it within your power to protect her from life's pain but that you held back, so she becomes furious and blames you for allowing her to be wounded. Her expectations of you, of course, are completely unrealistic.

Another factor in this dynamic is that you both have a strong identification with each other as females. The mother-daughter relationship is deep. You have a huge influence over her life. Your daughter is trying to understand her story, why she is the way she is. There is often a push-pull as your daughter is working to define herself.

That was part of what Hannah's outburst was really about—trying to define herself and find her place in her family and the world.

## Why It's Hard

Do you remember what you were like in your twenties? You knew everything and your mom knew nothing. I shudder at some of the bigheaded things I said to my mom in my twenties.

When your daughter initiates (springs) this conversation (outburst) with (on) you, she's typically coming from an "I know better than you" place. Part of this comes from the arrogance of youth. The other part, as we've discussed, is the immature brain, which attacks with a binary good-bad, all-or-nothing lens.

"You never spent time with me."

"You were never around."

"You were always on me."

"I couldn't do anything right."

In contrast, the mature brain sees things from several perspectives and therefore would have a more holistic story. Missing the nuance for now, your daughter combines her myopic take with arrogance and inexperience, and so she feels more than righteous attacking you and pronouncing her story (full of gross generalizations) as truth.

But what really knocks us off our horse and makes this exchange so difficult for moms is how the story is initiated—out of nowhere. John Gottman, PhD, a psychological researcher who studies human inter-action, would call this a "harsh startup." He examined harsh startups in his 1999 *New York Times*–bestselling book, *The Seven Principles for Making Marriage Work*. Harsh startups come at you like machine gun fire, a steady stream of criticisms, judgments, and accusations, leaving no room for response. You feel blasted. Not to mention, you expected things would get better as she got older. (In contrast, Gott-man's "soft startup" is a respectful and congenial conversation that leaves out the criticism.)

If you're like most moms, throughout your daughter's high school years you felt underappreciated and misunderstood. You looked for-ward to her leaving home, experiencing the world, and finally getting it. You fantasized about her saying, "Wow, Mom, I don't know how you did it all. I'm sorry I wasn't more grateful," or "I'm so sorry I was such a slob. Now that I'm living with a messy roommate, I get it."

There's a part of you waiting for appreciation. You want her to acknowledge how much you sacrificed for her. You want to be recognized and seen. Sometimes this does happen. When it does, it feels like a choir of angels is singing with a full-blown orchestra in surround sound.

But when you have this secret hope to be appreciated and you get blasted instead—well, it's horrible. It feels like your daughter has thrown a hand grenade into your heart. You feel the pain of being misunderstood, wrongly blamed, and judged by her. Her accusations threaten your identity as a mom. You start to question if you're a good mom, and then you go all in on shame.

This conversation is hard because it stirs up intense feelings for both you and your daughter.

## How You Make It Harder

So, your daughter has just laid into you. Now what? All the warning lights in your lower brain are flashing. You feel the blood pumping and the adrenaline surging. You can't help it; you get defensive and fire back with more all-or-nothing statements:

"That's not true. I was there for you."

"You were my life. I sacrificed everything for you."

"All the vacations I took you on. I sent you to a private high school, and I'm paying for your college. All the meals I made. All the times I cleaned up after you. I've done so much for you."

And you may say to yourself, what's wrong with that? I'm just defending myself.

But what you're doing is heightening the emotion and entering the stress response of fight. In about half a second, "defending yourself" turns into a full-fledged counterattack: "You say I was never there for you. That's your fault, missy. You were horrible in high school. You were mean, ugly, and entitled. I can't believe I raised such an ungrateful child."

To which, your daughter—now joining you in fight mode—responds: "See, Mom? That's what I'm talking about. You never listen. It's always about you. You're the one who's mean."

So you throw it right back at her with a cheap apology: "I'm sorry you think I'm a terrible mom. I'm sorry you aren't mature enough to understand what it means to be an adult. I'm sorry you're so sensitive. I'm sorry, but you were very disrespectful in high school."

And then make your point hit home by mocking her: "Oh, you're right, I never did anything for you." Or, "If you're so smart, why aren't you making straight As in your classes?" Or, "Oh, I guess paying $50,000 a year for tuition is doing nothing for you." Or you can take the more subtle approach to making your point—and making things worse—by ignoring your daughter completely.

## Turn a Hard Conversation
## Into a Healing Conversation

In case you're wondering, yes, I've had a hard conversation with my daughter.

My daughter was sixteen months old when I divorced her dad. I wanted her to have a good relationship with him. But as she entered middle school and then high school, things between them became more strained. It got to a point where my daughter would only have coffee once a week with her dad at Starbucks, and she wanted me there. It wasn't until she was nineteen that traumatic memories from her childhood started to surface, and she cut him off completely.

Fast-forward to when my daughter was twenty-two and she met me in Carmel, California. We spent several days together driving through Big Sur, discovering beaches, and going on a whale watching tour. The last day of our visit, we sat on our balcony watching the sunset. I was halfway through a glass of chardonnay when she unleashed. Truly, I can't even remember what she said because I went straight to shock. But the gist of it was that I hadn't protected her. She was angry that I made her see her dad. I was hurt. I felt misunderstood. I was so upset that tears ran down my cheeks. The last thing I ever would have done was intentionally hurt my daughter.

In that moment, I got defensive and that got us absolutely nowhere. I told my daughter, "I didn't know those bad things happened when you were little. How could you be mad at me?" This made my daughter angrier. I felt defeated and heartbroken. We somehow got through that night and grabbed some dinner. But the words that were spoken were like sharp knives hanging over my head the entire evening.

It wasn't until the next day as I drove to the airport that I could get past my defensive thoughts (get past myself), become curious about my daughter, and start the process of turning this hard conversation into a healing one. First, I revisited her words and tried to see what she was saying from her perspective. I then asked myself why she would bring this up and why now. It felt like such a blow to our usually good relationship. Though I felt attacked, I knew she wasn't being mean. I realized that she was offering me a gift. There was a wound, and she didn't want that to be between us. Underneath her anger was hurt that I hadn't protected her.

Then, I asked myself if there was any truth to what she said. And this is the hardest part. I'm a therapist; I should be the perfect parent, right? But I knew if our relationship was going to heal, I had to own my part. I had to admit where I let her down. I didn't have to own her whole story, but I needed to take responsibility for my portion.

I was still driving when it hit me. Unintentionally and while doing the best I knew how at the time, I hadn't protected my daughter as much as I could have. Her feelings were valid. I realized that I had blind spots and issues of my own when it came to her father. I was afraid of him. I would freeze up around him. I didn't want to make waves, so I accommodated him and didn't confront him as much as I should have.

I wrote my daughter a heartfelt apology. I didn't defend myself. I kept it focused on her. I told her how sorry I was, and how I wished I'd done it differently. I shared my new insights and took responsibility.

It was scary for me to send that because I had no idea how she would respond. But a day later, my daughter wrote me back and graciously accepted my apology. She told me it meant the world to her. My daughter felt seen and understood. She also shifted how she saw me. She began to see me as a human being with vulnerabilities. I was no longer the therapist mom on a pedestal.

This experience brought us closer together. It wasn't about me being right or the perfect mom. It wasn't about me at all. This hard-conversation-turned-healing-conversation was about her heal-ing past hurts. That's what I wanted most of all, and such healing could only happen when I got my ego out of the way.

## Six Keys to a Healing Conversation

Expectation and preparation are key to turning a hard conversation into a healing one. Next time your daughter starts slinging the accusa-tions at you, steady yourself and follow these six keys to supporting your daughter in processing and healing her childhood wounds and traumas.

### 1. Have a Clear Motive

When your daughter initiates a hard conversation, though it feels like she's attacking you, remember her motive isn't to hurt you, so there's no need for your motive to be defense. She's trying to make sense of her life struggles and figure out why things are the way they are. She's tired of feeling anxious, stuck, unhappy, and lonely. Though she's yell-ing at you, what she wants is to move forward and be happy. Even when you disagree with the story she's telling, your motive must be to support her effort here. When her healing is your North Star, you'll find it's easy to break through the hard and get to the good.

### 2. Slow It Down

When your daughter is emotionally flooded and comes at you with the harsh startup, it's like thirty-five bucking bulls have just been let out of the gate. Your daughter is venting in all directions, and it's not productive for her or you.

Your job here becomes to slow her down. That can be as easy as saying, "I'm a little overwhelmed. Could you slow it down so that I can fully take in what you're saying? When you said I don't care about you, what do you mean? I really want to understand. I don't want to miss what you're saying."

This will not only help you to hear her, but also help her to hear herself.

## 3. Listen with Curiosity

If we're honest, most of us listen only to prove our point: we listen not to hear but to find evidence that the other person is wrong and we're right. You can tell you're listening defensively when you constantly interrupt to make corrections. This is especially true when we're "listening" to our daughters. We're their mothers after all. But when we listen with the certainty that we're right, we close ourselves off to new information. We make quick interpretations without knowing the whole story.

If the goal is to seek understanding, then the way to listen is with curiosity and with the motive of your daughter's healing. Ask questions about what you don't understand or check out your assumptions with more open-ended questions:

- "What was it like for you when I started dating your stepdad?"
- "Tell me why you hated your high school."
- "Where did you feel that I was hard on you?"
- "Can you tell me why you felt I liked your older sister more?"
- "How do these experiences impact you now?"

It takes humility to stay open and not make quick judgments. But you want to understand her story, her feelings, and the significance of them on her life and future. What was her experience like? Where are her blind spots? What information is she missing? Where is her immaturity prohibiting her from understanding you?

Being right is overrated. Listening with curiosity brings healing and draws you closer.

## 4. Take Time

Be prepared. It's rare a hard conversation transforms into a healing conversation the first time your daughter opens the floodgates. Typically, it takes several attempts. Here's why: Even when you know these hard conversations are going to happen, you're still likely to be caught off guard when your daughter opens the floodgates. Suddenly, you're awash in herculean emotions like alarm, anger, sadness, and defensiveness that won't let you listen well. You automatically go into the stress response. Your lower brain takes control. If you attempt a conversation at this point, you'll only make things worse.

Take the time needed to regain your emotional balance and find your way back to calm. Reconnect to your higher brain, where the faculties you need to transform the conversation reside.

To get back to that place of balance, meditate, go running, journal, garden, play guitar, pray, call a friend, take a nap, or find a distraction like shopping. (You want to stay away from alcohol because numbing your feelings isn't the same as getting back to calm. The numbness is a false veil that can quickly slip when matters get heated.)

As you make your way back to calm, use the time to acknowledge your feelings. If fear comes up (and it probably will), journal about what the specific fear is. If the tears come, don't hold them back. This allows you to release the strong emotions from feeling attacked. It's important that you validate your emotions for yourself because your daughter can't. She needs you to focus on her healing, not your feelings.

Use this time to reflect on what just happened. Again, get curious. Why was my daughter so upset? Why did I react so strongly? What are my feelings telling me? What was my daughter trying to tell me? In other words, use this time to get perspective and get clear about the questions you'd like to ask her.

So, in the heat of the moment, how do you tell your angry, snapping daughter that you need this time? What won't work is if you just walk away and shut the bedroom door. This likely will escalate her desperation for you to understand her. She will read the closed door as evidence that you don't care. Instead, say something like this: "Dear, I hear this is really important to you and that you're really upset. I want to be honest with you that I'm feeling overwhelmed and I'm having a hard time listening to you well. What you're saying is so important that I don't want to misunderstand. I need some time to think about what you've said. Can we talk about this again after dinner?"

Then take the initiative and bring it up when you're ready.

## 5. Own Your Part

When you do bring it up, start by letting your daughter clarify what she said (that is, what she accused you of). Then, own your part. Find in her story something you agree with. I know, big ask. But you want her to know you're trying to understand her feelings. "I can see how our moving in your junior year would've been hard. You had to leave your close friends and start over."

Here's where you earn your PhD in listening. You've already learned to go from defensive listening to listening with curiosity. Now listen for where you may have consciously or unconsciously contributed to her situation. You don't have to agree with the whole story (but don't tell her that yet). Just find part of the story you can affirm.

To help keep your defensiveness at bay, think in terms of percentages. Even if your daughter is ninety-nine percent to blame in this situation, what's your one percent? Or even if you think it's pretty much a hundred percent her dad's fault, is there even a half a percent that might belong to you?

Owning some of the blame, seeing some truth in what she says, doesn't mean you're a horrible mom. It means you're human. Parenting is hard, and the right thing to do isn't always obvious. Don't make excuses for yourself. Just own up to your part so her healing can begin.

## 6. Offer a Heartfelt Apology

Once you own your part, you can offer a heartfelt apology—the thing that ultimately turns a hard conversation into a healing one. A heartfelt apology has the power to transform pain into insight and empathy.

A heartfelt apology is sincere. It is honest. It's not about you. It's focused on your daughter. You apologize for how you contributed to her difficulty. You own your part. You acknowledge how this impacted her: "Dear, I'm so sorry. You're right. I wasn't sensitive to how hard this move was for you. I did minimize how it would affect you. I realize just telling you to be more social wasn't helpful at all. It made you feel worse. I wish I had been more tuned in to you at this time."

You don't apologize with the expectation of her reciprocating. And you don't over-apologize either. Saying something like "I'm so sorry I ruined your life" is not helpful because it's not true.

With a heartfelt apology, you give her the gift of empathy and understanding. As Dr. Harriet Lerner wrote in her book *Why Won't You Apologize?*, "If only our passion to understand the other person were as great as our passion to be understood. Were this so, all of our apologies would be truly meaningful and healing."

Once the heartfelt apology has been given and some time has passed, only then should you lovingly explain to your daughter where your story differed from hers and why. "Dear, there are some things you need to know. Your dad was about to be laid off. We were going into debt. I didn't want to move either. Your dad and I were not on the same page. We were getting into a lot of fights. Here's where we see things differently: I didn't move to ruin your life. We moved so we could survive as a family. This doesn't take away from your experience at all. I still could have been more sensitive to you."

Done well, these conversations allow your daughter to see there's more to the story (and every story) than she understood as a child. She comes to realize that the world isn't simple and that whatever the outcome, your intentions were always the best—making her feel even closer to you.

Conversations such as these are possible with an emerging adult because they have more capacity for empathy and perspective than they had as teens. These conversations are real teaching moments and offer important glimpses into the adult world.

I remember decades ago sitting around the kitchen table with my mom and her mom, my nana. I loved hearing the real stories that included struggle and hardship because it helped me understand them. Like how Nana was widowed in the Great Depression, lost a child to pneumonia, and what it took to raise my mom alone. It was eye-opening for sure, but it modeled something so significant to me about the richness and importance of being authentic. Those times taught me more about empathy than anything else. It taught me that most of the time, we only see the tip of the iceberg in any given situation. There's so much more to people's story than meets the eye.

## Why Healing Conversations Are Worth It

Turning a hard conversation into a healing conversation is not easy to do. Our egos can flare and we can armor up in a half second. This is why it's important to remind ourselves why healing conversations are worth it.

- It's healing for her, for you, and for your relationship.

- It helps her grow up—she sees that life isn't easy, tough choices have to be made, and sometimes wrong choices get made.

- You model the very mature behavior of owning up to blind spots and errors, intentional or unintentional.

- You teach her it's not about being right. This is not a win-lose game. Life is not binary, all good or bad, or all your fault or all my fault. It's about curiosity, understanding, and the humility to admit you don't know the whole story.

- You model owning your part and taking responsibility for it.

- You show that laying aside your ego opens the space for empathy for the other.

- You help her to understand that you are a human being who is not perfect and doesn't always know what to do. In other words, you are not a mom-bot. You don't know everything.

- You give her permission to be imperfect and at a loss for what to do when she faces hard choices too. You let her see that there is no perfect decision, only the better decision.

- With your apology and the understanding she gains from it, you eliminate her ability to blame you. She can now see that she must assume responsibility for how she heals or manages her issues from here.

- You teach her that it's always possible to turn a hard conversation into a healing conversation. And that it's possible to maintain connection even when you disagree.

Though not the most pleasant part of your daughter's journey to adulthood, these hard-to-healing conversations are worth all the energy you put into them. Most especially because they result in a deeper, more trusting, more honest relationship between you and your daughter, now and for years to come.

## Exercise: Practice the Six Keys to Healing

THE BEST THING you can do to turn your next hard conversation into a healing conversation is to prepare your brain. Think back to the last hard conversation (blowout) you and your daughter had. Then, re-create it in your journal as a healing conversation by walking it through the six keys. Step by step, note what you'd be thinking (and not thinking); doing (and not doing); saying (and not saying)...

1 Have a clear motive.
2 Slow it down.
3 Listen with curiosity.
4 Take time.
5 Own your part.
6 Offer a heartfelt apology.

Thinking this through ahead of time helps you to be prepared for the next out-of-nowhere confrontation. Healing conversations take practice. No worries though; if experience is any indication, your daughter is likely to give you plenty. And now, you're ready to receive each conversation as the opportunity it is to bring you closer.

# 8

# The Mom Crisis

M Y COLLEAGUE and trusted friend Sara and I have met for lunch at least once a month consistently since graduate school—more than twenty years. I think she's the best marriage and family therapist in town, and she feels the same about me.

Sara is typically upbeat, confident, and amazingly present. But several years ago at one of our lunches, she was different. Things seemed off. Her energy was flat, and she was withdrawn.

"Are you okay?" I asked.

"I just don't feel needed," she said.

"What do you mean? You see a ridiculous number of clients each week. You have a waiting list," I replied.

"It's not about work, it's about Braden and Kelsey. They have their own people now." (Braden is her twenty-three-year-old son, and Kelsey is her twenty-five-year-old daughter.)

"What do you mean 'they have their own people'?" I asked.

"Well, now that Braden is engaged to be married, he confides in Ella. And Kelsey is such a happy newlywed. Of course, her go-to person now is Michael. I couldn't be happier. It's everything I ever wanted for them. But it's also really hard. Especially with Kelsey. I was her external emotional regulator on a daily basis. Now, all I can do is wonder how she's doing. That leaves me feeling anxious," Sara said.

"Hold on. Can you say in plain English what an 'external emotional regulator' is?" I asked.

Sara laughed. "Okay. Kelsey would check in with me every day. She'd ask for my opinion on what she should do at work or how to handle boyfriends, anything and everything. She'd call me when she was stressed and needed to vent or when she had good news. She'd text just to tell me she bought a cute pair of jeans. To be honest, I loved giving her my opinion, encouraging her, or helping her relax. But I'm not that person anymore, she has Michael . . . and they don't even need me financially. I can't believe I'm saying that." She smiled.

I heard what Sara said. But I didn't get it, not really. At that time, I was still my daughter's daily "external emotional regulator," so I couldn't truly empathize with Sara. I may have even been a little envious.

Seven years later, I get it. My daughter is in love, and I think he is "the one." I like him a lot. And he has become her person. I no longer know how she's feeling or what's happening on a daily basis. I don't feel needed in the same way, because I'm not needed in the same way. It feels super disorienting and brings up a deep sorrow. Yet it also makes me happy to see her living her life fully. This is, after all, what I truly want for her. In many ways, I feel closer to her than ever.

You'd think a couple of seasoned family therapists would be overjoyed that their kids are happy, financially stable, and have found their people. Isn't this what we've been working toward our daughters' whole lives?

Of course! Then why does their independence shake us to the core? Because when our children become independent of us, it's a whole other level of letting go. It's the Mom Crisis.

## The Paradox of the Mom Crisis

Seeing your daughter finally launched and functioning well in the world without you is a big change. Part of you knows this is healthy and normal; another part feels like your world is ending. You are at once overjoyed and jolted. And the tension caused by these simultaneous, opposite emotions in your brain can feel confusing and uncomfortable.

Recognize that even with positive change, there's grief. You've invested a significant amount of your heart, soul, time, energy, attention, and years into raising your daughter. "Mom" has been your identity. So when you feel the loss of that identity—an identity you loved—it can throw you into a bit of a tailspin.

*But she hasn't lived under my roof for years*, you're probably thinking. *Why am I having this crisis now?*

The Mom Crisis doesn't happen when your daughter turns eighteen and leaves home. Yes, you felt the pang of letting go, but for the first couple of years, you felt needed. When your daughter hit the road to independence, she probably encountered quite a few bumps, especially in those early years, and turned to you for help weathering them. On a regular basis, she called you into her life. Your key facets and your consultant hat were always at the ready.

Now, finally, and in no small part thanks to your guidance, she's become competent at avoiding major bumps and better at navigating others on her own. She's independent. The irony here is this is the day you've been waiting for. She has her people, she's on her path, and she doesn't even need your money!

This is cause for celebration. But it's also a time of transition, and thus, you feel grief. Grief doesn't mean there's anything wrong. It's a natural response to change. For more than two decades, your relationship with your daughter has been relevant and fulfilling (even if the last few years were trying). Now, she doesn't need you the same way she did, and you're unsure of where you fit in her life going forward—leaving you rather lost at this moment.

One mom described it to me as "feeling irrelevant." She said, "I can't believe I'm actually missing things that I used to complain about. So much of my life was focused on her. Of course, I miss the good times. But now, I almost miss the drama. Between her grades, friends, broken curfews, and empty White Claw cans in her room, she was constantly on my mind. The other day, I realized I not only miss her physical presence, I miss her in my head. Without all the preoccupation and worry, my head feels like an empty auditorium."

This emptiness can feel like a death, and in some sense it is. Your daughter is stepping into adulthood, and your role as mom is entering a new phase. Even if you have a career, tons of friends, and a full life outside your daughter, this transition leaves a hole in your life.

## Was I a Good Mom?

When that auditorium opens up in our own heads, we moms start running around in it, trying to make sense of the last two decades of our lives. We ask ourselves: "Will my daughter be okay?" "Could I have done more?" "Was I a good mom or a bad mom?"

After all, moms don't have supervisors. We don't even get a training manual. All other jobs come with immediate feedback from clients, products, financials, and managers. You get year-end reviews and bonuses. You receive validation. When you sacrifice, you're rewarded. When your job changes or you get promoted, you're notified. Maybe you even get a raise.

But being the mom of a daughter approaching adulthood... sheesh. You're starving for a teaspoon of appreciation and validation, not to mention some pointers from somebody, anybody, who knows what to do. Then, when she can finally manage life on her own (a sure sign you've done something well) and your job is changing, all you get is left in the dark. Nobody hands you a gold watch or gives you a trip to Hawaii.

You are left in that empty auditorium to judge yourself.

Remember in *The Wizard of Oz* when Glinda asks Dorothy, "Are you a good witch or a bad witch?" It's easy to answer that in the movie. You're a bad witch if you're the one with a green face and talk in a crackling voice. And you're a good witch if you're gorgeous, wear a ginormous white ball gown, and talk with a soothing tone. I think all moms have days when we feel like the bad witch and maybe our faces even turn green. Other days, we definitely are Glinda the Good Witch, absent the tiara, white dress, and wand.

But parenting is not made of binary (good or bad) choices, so it's not useful to think of it that way. What is being a "good mom" anyway? Are you a good mom if your daughter is successful? Okay then, what's your definition of success? If you define success as both you and your daughter getting everything right... how do you define right?

Drill down into this desire to be considered the perfect parent (a desire too many of us lug around), and you'll see that it isn't even possible. Perfection is a societal construct. What's deemed "good" is a social construct. And your relationship to your daughter is unique and real.

## No One Gets Out of Motherhood Unscathed

Most moms would say that motherhood is a life-enriching experience they wouldn't trade for the world. However, no mom on this planet would say, "These past twenty years of mothering my daughter have been pure bliss." No one comes out of this mothering venture unscathed. It's way more difficult than any of us ever imagined. The feelings left from unresolved difficulties are part of what we're wrestling with and what's causing the Mom Crisis.

When we were in the parenting trenches, we didn't have time to be reflective about the pain that came with the job. We were so focused on raising our kids that we didn't have time to grapple with the thousands of slights we absorbed over two decades. So now, as we transition out of active parenting, we find ourselves haunted by voices like Gollum's in *The Lord of the Rings*, whispering in our ear past wounds, disappointments, and resentments.

When you first hold your baby, you're giddy with high expectations. You anticipate a bright and promising future together. Then life happens. She isn't the mini-me you imagined. She's her own person. And the minute she learns the word *no*, she starts pushing against you to become that person. While that may be natural, and it may be what we all pray for as parents, it still hurts.

As all women know (because we were once girls), girls can be mean. Especially to their mothers. We've all been at the receiving end of careless words, cumulative entitlement, back talk, and disrespect. "I hate you." "I hope you die." "No wonder Daddy left you."

Not all the attacks are as direct, however. Sometimes it's her choices that wound us:

- not wanting to be around you
- lying to your face
- defying values that are sacred to you
- deciding to live with dad and not you

Then come the disappointments. They start early. At first, you want your precious little four-year-old to wear a beautiful dress, and she makes it clear she's wearing her favorite T-shirt and jeans. As she grows, the disappointments (and your level of worry) only build in seriousness:

- If you want her to pursue music, she wants to pursue soccer.

- If you want her to be outgoing and popular, she's shy and comfortable with having one best friend.

- If you want your daughter to be on the dance team, she is into anime.

- If you went to medical school and academics are important to you, she decides to be a hairdresser.

- If going to church is important to you, she tells you she doesn't believe in God.

When these wounds and disappointments are left unprocessed, they produce resentment. We wonder if the years and time we've given to raising our daughter were worth it (not that we'd have had it any other way). From there, we move on to "I failed" and "I don't matter."

My client Mary was a stay-at-home mom. When I asked how her daughter Camille, now a junior in college, was doing, Mary replied, "Oh, she's great. She's doing a semester abroad in Spain, learning Spanish. She's having the time of her life."

"And you?" I asked.

"I'm struggling. I still manage to run every day, but I don't feel essential anymore. I feel useless. My husband thinks I should get a job. Of course, he was the one who thought I should quit work to be a stay-at-home mom. Before we had kids, I was doing great in my career and making more money than him. Now what do I have?"

Though I would never have pointed it out to her in that moment, Mary had a lot. She had a daughter well on her way to independence, a successful marriage, her health, and the rest of her life in front of her. My job here was to help Mary see all that for herself eventually. But in that moment, on the precipice of the Mom Crisis, Mary was deep into what I call her Mom Story.

## Your Mom Story

The Mom Story is the story we tell ourselves about our parenting journey thus far. When we are in the Mom Crisis stage of parenting, all those unprocessed wounds and disappointments, now turned into resentments, take the starring roles in this first draft of our tale.

You tell this story to yourself in bits and pieces, and craft it mostly in your unconscious—so you never really consider the whole story. Your mind highlights the parts that serve your Mom Crisis—and those are the stories that always get told. Other parts, your mind skips over. Some parts are deleted entirely. Most detrimental to your seeing the full truth of your parenting tale is that this first draft only contains one perspective: yours.

The more you tell this first draft of your story or let it roll around in your head, the more locked into it you become. When you share what your daughter did or didn't do with your most trusted friends, of course they nod in agreement and take your side. As much as you love the validation, know that every nod serves to cement this first draft, until you're trapped in a story that is missing critical information and doesn't serve you or your daughter well.

Stories are how we interpret our lives. When they are limited, we limit ourselves. A story that focuses on past hurts keeps us vacillating between making either ourselves or our daughter the villain. It keeps us in a cycle of judgment and shame.

There is, however, another way to tell this story. A second draft that's more comprehensive and can expand your possibilities. By including the whole story, a good second draft honors where you and your daughter have been, where you've struggled, where you've triumphed, and where you're headed next together. In doing so, it relieves the Mom Crisis and releases both you and your daughter from past transgressions. To get to that second draft, however, we must begin by bringing our first draft into our consciousness, where we can look at it critically.

## Healing Our Wounds—Digging in Our Dirt

When we make the unconscious conscious, it becomes the gateway to fresh insights and awareness, personal growth, and limitless possibilities. Neurologically speaking, this integrates the limbic system of the lower brain (that stores strong emotional memories and trauma) with the higher brain (where memories and trauma can come into consciousness). The best the lower brain can do is to create a partial story (a first draft). When we move this partial story into our awareness and view it from the expansiveness of the cortex in the higher brain, only then can we create a new holistic, helpful, and life-generating second draft of our story.

I help clients, like Mary, bring that partial story into their consciousness and write out the first draft of their Mom Story using three prompts, which are listed with explanations and directions in the section to follow. As soon as you finish this chapter, I encourage you to use these prompts and begin your first draft. You can write in your journal. Or if you like, you can download the "First Draft Worksheet"—which has the prompts right on it—at colleenogrady.com/dialupthe dreamworksheets.

As you move through the prompts, don't edit yourself; don't worry about grammar. Write what feels true right now. Include any words you like (even ones that begin with the letter "F").

Don't expect this to be pretty. It won't be. These prompts will lead you to dig deep into your own dirt. But as you go deeper, you'll discover this soil is rich for releasing, healing, and finding peace within yourself. Also, the good soil you till here will produce fruits that will nourish both you and your daughter as you move into this next phase of parenting and life.

## Bringing Your First Draft to Awareness

### Prompt 1: What was hard about parenting your daughter? Where were you disappointed?

When we're around other parents we don't know well, we often filter our parenting story. We don't talk about the hard stuff because we don't want to be judged. But as a therapist, I've heard decades of hard stories. I know there's plenty to be grateful for, and we'll get to that in the next chapter. But for right now, I want you to write out what was hard about mothering and the times you felt disappointed.

One of my clients told me how her daughter was late for curfew. Mom grew increasingly panicked until her daughter stumbled in drunk at 4 a.m., at which time she unleashed all her anxiety and fear onto her daughter. "How could you do this to me? Do you know what you put me through?"

Though Mom was understandably emotional and concerned for her daughter's well-being, this was the absolute wrong time to have this conversation. The drunken daughter—not so concerned for herself or her mother—laughed and flipped her mom off.

Though the daughter has, of course, grown out of such reckless, callous behavior, the lack of empathy she showed that night never got resolved and so continued to fester inside Mom.

This is your time to get out those hurts. Write out everything that you felt your daughter did to you and put you through. You may have been scared. You may have been humiliated. Write down every disappointment you faced as a parent—big and small. Where your daughter disappointed you, where you think you disappointed her, where you disappointed yourself, and any disappointments life handed you and your daughter along the way. You may have been betrayed. You may have been furious. Write it down. If it's easier to list in bullet points, do that. Write until you can't think of anything else.

When I did this exercise, I found it incredibly validating. Even though your husband, friends, or teen can't empathize with the depth of what you're feeling, you can validate yourself. You get to name your experience, tell your truth, and view it from a place of compassion. You get to see in black and white that it was hard.

Let the feelings come up. Welcome the tears. You're releasing emotions that you've carried inside yourself for years. You're likely to discover a newfound empathy for your life as a mom.

I wish I were physically there with you. I'd give you a huge hug. If from this prompt you see or feel that you're stuck in some memory, feeling depressed, or experiencing trauma, I encourage you to see a therapist to help you work through these memories and unhealed wounds.

## Prompt 2: Where do you beat yourself up?

What do you regret? Where did you fail? Write it down.

I want you to answer these prompts not to make you feel worse about yourself, but for you to expose that whispering Gollum voice: "You are a failure." "Shame on you."

Most moms have a parenting moment they're not proud of... or maybe a parenting season. This haunts us when we see that our daughter is not doing well. We lie awake at night wondering if we really did ruin her life.

I'll never forget my first case as an intern. Roberta had been seeing psychiatrists for thirty years, and her file was as thick as a Houston phone book. I was very intimidated by her. She had a horrible past. She was angry and told me straight out that she literally threw her baby in a Dumpster. I was in way over my head with Roberta and became tongue-tied. In front of my supervisor, psychiatry residents, and fellows, watching from behind a one-way mirror, she stood up and screamed at me, "You ruined my life!" Her words shook me to my core at first. I had no idea what to say. One of my hidden fears about becoming a therapist was that I would ruin someone's life. But in retrospect, I realized Roberta had given me a huge gift. She put my hidden fear right out in the world where I could see the absurdity of it. Obviously I couldn't and didn't ruin her life after a couple of sessions.

I can tell you that you haven't ruined your daughter's life either. But to get free of Gollum's voice, I want you to answer my prompts and look for your part in creating what you regard as regrets and failures in your parenting.

Did you ever escalate things with your daughter? Did you ever ignore her or what she was doing? Could you have handled things differently? Did you ever offload your stress and worries onto her? Were your expectations unreasonable? Did you get so caught up in monitoring your daughter that you missed out on really knowing her? Did your ego get in the way? Did you accept your daughter for who she is or were you trying to make her more like you? Were you ashamed of her because she made you look bad? Did you get frustrated with her because she took up so much time and got in the way of your work? Do you regret how you talked to her? Did you label or threaten her when you were frustrated or scared?

Don't worry if you answer yes to these questions. It doesn't mean you're a bad mother. If you told me you did nothing wrong and have no regrets, then I'd worry. Because moms are human, we blow it sometimes. The things you regret are not all your daughter's fault and they're not all your fault either. But to heal them, you must courageously and honestly own your part.

I was speaking at the National Conference on Adolescents and Young Adults for mental health professionals. After my presentation, a seasoned licensed professional counselor approached me and told me that her daughter was thirty-two and she'd been estranged from her for ten years. She told me, "She won't talk to me."

I told her to leave a message for her daughter to say that she'd gone to my workshop, had some new insights into their relationship, and wanted to own her part.

The next morning, I was in the line at Starbucks when the counselor tapped me on the shoulder. "I did what you said. I left that message, and she called me back immediately. We had a really good talk."

By exploring these prompts, you'll see you didn't ruin her life, but you did have a part to play in some of the drama.

### Prompt 3: Release and forgive.

Just answering these prompts, acknowledging your disappointments and perceived failures, and feeling your feelings can be a big release for you. However, there's one last step you must take to get from this first draft to a healing second draft. Finish these two statements:

1 I forgive my daughter for...
2 I forgive myself for...

At this point, I'm not asking you to do anything but write. I'm not asking you to talk to your daughter or offer your forgiveness to her right now. So, when you write, be as honest and as specific as you can because it will make it more meaningful.

Close your eyes and take a few minutes here. Say the statement you're working on out loud: "I forgive my daughter for..." or "I forgive myself for..." Write whatever comes to mind. Keep writing until you feel it's complete.

Your Mom Story may have already shifted and changed a bit. Bring those new insights into your writing here. Statements like "I forgive my daughter for being such an entitled brat" or "I forgive myself for being such an idiot" are first-draft thinking. If you can include the *why* of what happened in your forgiveness statement, you are starting to see things in a bigger context and moving into second-draft thinking. For instance, "I forgive my daughter for being so angry. I see now that I put high expectations on her and never took the time to listen to her, which contributed to that." Or, "I forgive myself because I really wanted the best for her, and I was super stressed at that time with the demands at work and with my sister in the hospital."

Once you finish writing this first draft of your Mom Story, you might feel a little lighter, a little more connected to yourself, and find a lot more self-compassion. We can't change our past, but we can change how we frame it. We have to learn to accept what was and what is. Once in that headspace, we can write a second draft that honors where we've been and that motivates us as we move forward.

## Accept and Let Go

Your daughter has a lot of transitions of her own ahead. She'll be turning to you and your wisdom and love to see her through. Part of preparing yourself to be there for her is fully accepting your parenting journey thus far, understanding it in all its facets, and even appreciating it.

Now, when you feel that emptiness and loss of purpose—aka, the Mom Crisis—you can see it as an opportunity to process your parenting journey thus far. To relive the good times. Pat yourself on the back for getting through the bad times. Process the pain. And prepare yourself for this next phase.

And just so you know—if you want to give yourself that gold watch and trip to Hawaii for a job well done, go for it.

## Exercise: A Ritual for Letting Go

THE PASSAGES in our lives deserve ritual. Yet ritual is so often missing in parenting these days. But just because there's no ceremony for when we transition out of parenting every moment of every day, doesn't mean we can't create one for ourselves.

1   Once your first draft of your Mom Story is on paper, sit with it and ask: Is this version of my story helpful? Is it working for me? Does it make me a better human being? Does it motivate me to be a better mom?

2   When you're ready, make a copy of what you've written on the "First Draft Worksheet" or in your journal. (You're going to want to keep the original for reference later.)

3  Then, burn it. This little ceremony is a statement that you're letting go of this one-dimensional first draft, that you're ready for a new story, a second draft full of love, hope, and possibilities.

4  As you watch the words turn into ash and the smoke starts to rise, say something like this:

> I accept all of this—the hard, the heartbreak, the hurt, and the disappointment. I forgive my daughter and myself. We both were doing the best we could at the time. I choose to accept and love what is. I choose to honor my daughter and myself. I am open to a new story. I choose love over judgment. This is not the end; it's the beginning of a new chapter.

# 9

# Your Second Draft

---

FTER PROCESSING the pain, forgiving the missteps, and releasing the wounds in the first draft of her Mom Story, Mary felt relieved but somewhat adrift. She was grateful to be leaving past hurts in the past as she entered a new phase in her relationship with her daughter. But all the looking back had her wondering if she'd wasted the years when it came to her own development—if there'd been more loss than gain. She'd sacrificed so much for the family, and she didn't like who she was anymore. She longed for the time before kids, when she was at the top of her game.

But as I helped her take an objective look at what her job as Mom really entailed and produced, Mary experienced a huge mindset shift. She realized she'd been discounting her mothering as less important than being in corporate. "The ironic part," Mary told me, "is that the mothering job is ten times harder and took ten times the strategy of any corporate job."

I nodded my head and agreed. "Absolutely—so true!" I said. "It's common not to be conscious of the enormous skill set and level of competency required to parent well. The ultimate Powerless Parenting Message is that your mothering job is irrelevant in the big world, that your development has been on ice for eighteen years. It's a message our culture sends loud and clear." I sighed. "Like it doesn't count. It's not that important," I continued, my voice now getting louder. "The ultimate slam to mothers is that once you get your child across the adult finish line, and you have poured two hundred percent of your heart, soul, and mind into this venture, the corporate-business world and the patriarchal culture dismiss your work as immaterial. Like mothering took no talents, gifts, abilities, or brain cells to do. This is a total lie!"

Mary smiled. She could tell I was on a familiar rant.

## The Big Myth Exposed

Mary had bought into this ultimate Powerless Parenting Message. She just assumed the world was looking at her thinking, *You haven't worked in twenty years. What could you possibly have to offer? What could you possibly do?*

If you've bought into this message or think that your first draft of your Mom Story is the only version of that tale, it can feel like you've lost more than you've gained. You see your daughter in her prime, living her dream. But that's not what you see when you look in the mirror. You're no longer that young woman full of hope and idealism. You think, *Where did these wrinkles come from? What happened to my body? My daughter probably gave me gray hair, but thank God for hair color.* You romanticize the good old days before you had children. You may think it's too late for you now, that you missed your shot.

Mom, this is a big myth. It gets under our skin and makes us feel like an old, worn-out sofa that's been tossed to the curb on garbage day. Buying into this myth is dangerous to your vitality, health, and well-being. So you need to kick *it* to the curb. Replace it with the truth of what twenty years of parenting has brought to your life, also known as the second draft of your Mom Story.

As Mary worked on her second draft, she saw that parenting *is* *work*. And in doing that work, she'd acquired a long list of skills. She'd also acquired wisdom and grown as a person.

The second draft of Mary's Mom Story contained phrases like,

- If I could keep my disorganized and distracted daughter Camille on track, I can deal with disorganized vendors and employees.

- If I can stay calm and not react to a hormonal, crazed fifteen-year-old yelling at me, I can manage difficult employees with ease.

- I've had eighteen years of experience in successful diplomacy and conflict resolution. After all, I had to find a way to work things out with Camille. I couldn't simply fire her like she was an incompetent and annoying employee.

The next time we met, Mary shared that she'd decided to reenter the corporate world, and so we batted around a few ideas. "I know I'm a natural manager, but now I think I'd be great at sales too," she laughed. "Are you ever going to deal with a customer more resistant than a teenage girl? It's all marketing, after all. Daily, I had to find the right angle to elicit Camille's cooperation . . . I definitely have a whole new skill set because of being a mom."

With this new, fuller understanding of what she brought to the table, Mary started interacting with some contacts on LinkedIn and got a couple of interviews. No longer looking to corporate mores to validate her worth, she walked into those interviews knowing her value. She was offered a project manager position at a big firm and negotiated a six-figure salary before accepting.

Writing the second draft of your Mom Story is not about getting a corporate job (though, if that's what you want, it will definitely help). It's about comprehending, owning, and taking pride in who you've become. Respecting what you've accomplished and the insights you've gained. It's about knowing in your bones and in your heart that you're a better person because of being a mother.

## Bringing Your Second Draft to Consciousness

I see mothering as a mythic heroine's journey. Your first draft recounts the first leg of that journey, fraught with dangers and dark forces. There may have been times you thought you'd be taken out. But you're still here. And, I would add, stronger than ever.

Now that the battle has ceased, and the smoke has cleared, it's in this calm that you take a look at what's been won. You reexamine the places you've been and gather up the treasures left behind. Just as before, you might have to dig under a little debris to find the gold, but it's there.

As you learned in the last chapter, when done well, this second draft provides you with a more holistic story than the first draft. It doesn't leave anything out. You're not only recounting what happened, you're also processing it.

This second draft embraces with compassion the hard truths of the first draft. And then adds new truths about how you've expanded and deepened in the best possible way because of your experience being a mom. It recognizes how through the trials of motherhood, you've developed character, strength, and whole skill sets, just like Mary. The second draft opens your eyes to the good times, the busy times, the hard times, and the heartbreaks.

As with the first draft, before you begin working through the prompts in the section to follow, read through the rest of this chapter completely. When you are ready, write in your own notebook or journal or download the "Second Draft Worksheet" at colleenogrady.com/dialupthedreamworksheets and use it.

This second draft takes more mental energy and reflection to generate than the first draft did. So, set aside at least an hour to think through the prompts. (Think of this time as your own personal retreat.)

Some answers may come quickly, others not so much. You don't have to finish in one sitting. "I have no clue" is a perfectly acceptable response for your first attempt. You may even want to take a few days to reflect on certain prompts. The important thing here is to ponder these questions. However you approach them, know the answers will come. You may be in the shower or on a run when the flash of insight strikes. Be sure to write down your fresh aha moments as soon as possible.

I encourage you to give yourself the huge gift of writing out your answers completely, rather than in point form, for this second draft. I know you're super busy and facing a blank page can be daunting, but it's one thing to read the chapter and think through questions in your head and a completely different experience when you can see your gains written out on the page.

This second draft of your Mom Story is your personalized, unique, exceptional story. A story you can't fully own until you're fully aware of it—the good times and the hard. So, let's get started.

## Finding the Gold in the Good

In performing your normal, everyday responsibilities as a parent, you've added whole skill sets and grown in a myriad of ways. When you put a critical eye to all you took care of and all you accomplished in an average day as a mom, I dare you to be unimpressed. You'll see that this daily balancing act was not only an impressive management feat, but it stretched you, forced you out of your comfort zone, and helped you build all kinds of expertise. In excavating that growth, you unearth the gold. The following prompts will help you dig.

### Prompt 1: What hats did you wear?

What hats did you wear as you parented and managed your life, work, and household? What have you done well?

Here's what I know, you've worn a lot of hats in your life—and never more than when you were actively parenting. It would be nice if other family members noticed and maybe even asked, "Wow, how did you do it all?" But that's unlikely because doing it all was what was expected of you. Society—of which our family members are a part—puts unrealistic expectations on mothers. So often, the only time you got recognition is when you dropped the ball (like forgetting to pick up your daughter from early dismissal). So that's what gets highlighted in our brains and steals our focus from the hundred marvelous things we did on that same day.

It's time to change our perspective and take a realistic look at all the balls you kept in the air over two decades and the competence required to do that. Now that you aren't running around switching hats and costumes like a Marvel character, you can take the time to see that you not only handled multiple situations in a day, you were also learning and picking up new skills on the fly.

I don't think I've ever met a mom who said, "I am so proud of myself for all the hats I've worn as a mother and how successful I was in all those roles." Well, I want you to know I see you and your success. But more important, I want *you* to see yourself and revel in what it took to wear so many hats—and wear them well.

Make a list of all the roles you've played in your relationships, career, volunteer work, and your home. Here are some examples:

- your relationships: wife, mother, daughter, friend, sister, caregiver...

- your career: teacher, attorney, author, coach, CEO, pediatrician, accountant, corporate, entrepreneur, yoga instructor, physical therapist...

- your volunteer work: National Charity League, PTA, school fundraisers, mission trips, political campaigns, community service, food drives...

- your home: property manager, event planner, chef, financial planner, fix-it person, teacher, healthcare provider, housekeeper, gardener, decorator, personal shopper—I could go on all day.

### Prompt 2: What interpersonal skills did you hone?

As young moms, so many of us were determined to do it differently than our moms, meaning we'd "get it right." And we thought we knew what "right" was. That naivety is truly a grace. If we'd known the trials and tribulations ahead, well, we might have traded in our newborns.

We all bring natural abilities and qualities to mothering, but other abilities and qualities are called out of us, sometimes forged out of us, because that's what our daughters needed. It would have been so easy to parent them if they were just like us. We'd have known what to do if they were down, stressed, or defiant. We'd have the manual. But that just isn't how it works.

Our daughters are wired differently than we are, so our natural skill set only took us so far, and then we found ourselves enrolled in crash-course parenting 101, 201, 301...

I was a very sensitive child. Because my mom was overbearing, I would shut down. If my daughter had been like me, I would have instinctively known how to relate to her. I would be compassionate, empathic, and a thoughtful encourager. I would let her find her way and gently steer her if needed. I would give her lots of space and acceptance to express her opinions.

But as you've probably guessed by now, my daughter was not that girl. She did not shut down during conflict—or ever really. My daughter is strong. She fearlessly speaks her mind. She has opinions. Yes, there was a place for compassion, empathy, and encouragement in my parenting, but she needed more from me.

*I* needed to stop shutting down when confronted, develop a strong backbone, and take up my space. I needed to be one hundred percent clear and have an opinion. I needed to put on the brakes. And, at times, I needed to be able to contain her unruly, forceful rearing up and bucking as hard as she could. My daughter called gifts out of me that I didn't know I had. To parent her well and help her mature and use her strength wisely, I needed to find my own power to match hers.

What interpersonal skills and qualities have *you* developed through parenting? Here are some examples:

- your skills: organizing, protecting, counseling, managing, event planning, problem-solving, leadership, disciplinarian, cooking, diplomacy, negotiating, encouraging, strategizing, innovating, investigating...

- your qualities: compassionate, intuitive, wise, loving, kind, warm, joyful, steady, grounded, playful, fun, peaceful, energetic, calm, strong, determined, persevering, full of grit, logical, fierce, gentle, empathic…

Write them down.

## So Much Gold in the Good

To give you a sampling of all the ways motherhood develops and matures us, I asked my community of moms how they were better humans because of being a mom. Here are some of their answers:

- "I've learned to trust my gut. I'm not so selfish; I think about others more."

- "I'm deeper, more empathic, humbled, other-centered without being a martyr. I'm wiser."

- "I learned how to take a moment before responding to things. I have more self-control."

- "I now let go of things that don't matter. I have more understanding, and I'm more forgiving."

- "I'm less judgmental, more accepting, a better listener, and more curious."

- "My twenty-one-year-old daughter makes me want to be the version of me she thinks I am. Wise, strong, soft, constant, and a badass warrior in all things."

I know I am a much better therapist for having been a parent in the trenches instead of standing solely in my academic ivory tower. The same is true for my friend Ann.

Ann was a professor in early childhood development and was a consultant before she had kids. Her first pregnancy caused her to have to quit teaching and stay home. Then, she had two more babies in short succession, so she decided to stay home—at least while they were small. "It was a tough transition," she told me. "I felt like I'd lost my identity. Like, 'Am I still a person? Who am I?'"

With a house full of toddlers, Ann did manage a part-time position, in which she developed a children's ministry program by drawing on both her academic work and her new insights from parenting. Still, she worried she'd thrown away her chance for a full-time career in academia. Once the children were in school, she wanted to teach in college again, but with all those years off she thought it would be impossible.

And maybe it would have been. We'll never know because she created a better opportunity for herself—and it was a direct result of the insider knowledge she'd gained from being a mom. Parenting challenges were no longer academic to her. With the real-world expertise she'd gained from being a hands-on mom combined with her formal education, she founded Nurtured Noggins, where she is a parent coach and an early childhood development educator with a huge online presence. "Even though I was a childhood development expert before I had children," Ann explains, "I really didn't know anything until I experienced being a parent myself. I am now much more empathic and compassionate to other moms. I have the perspective that I was missing when I was a professor."

## Finding the Gold in the Hard

Sometimes the challenges we grow from aren't the too-much-to-do or trying-something-new kind. Sometimes it's the unexpected, the traumatic, or the thing that wears us down—the hard stuff—that causes us to evolve.

Think back to the most frustrating challenges you listed in the first draft of your Mom Story. The times when parenting your teen called for grit, strength, perseverance, and courage you didn't know you had. What lessons did you learn about yourself? How has this made you a better person?

Write them down. And then let's dig a little more.

## Prompt 3: How have you handled the unexpected and traumatic?

The one thing that's predictable and consistent about being a parent is that your best-laid plans will be interrupted and derailed, often by an unexpected, traumatic situation.

As I am writing this, it's been one year of dealing with the chaos and anxiety caused by Covid-19. Here's what I know: This completely unexpected pandemic drastically interrupted your life and your parenting. The longest spring break ever has turned into more than a year of your daughter's life being turned upside down.

As a mom, it's likely fallen to you to keep some type of normalcy in your home for your family while dealing with the pandemonium of online school (and all other versions) and week after week of uncertainty. On top of all that, you, like many of us, may have also dealt with natural disasters such as fires, freezes, or hurricanes.

Here's the deal, you can shake your fist at Covid-19, the weather, your husband who decided to leave you, the governor, the president, or God. But then you still have to figure it out. Moms don't have the luxury to feel sorry for themselves. You have to deal with it.

As mothers, we're pretty amazing at coming up with a plan to deal with the unexpected. Even when we're well past plan B—even when we've run out of letters in the alphabet—we keep trying. We rise from the ashes almost every day in hard times and put food on the table, figure out the finances, try to make things run smoothly in our homes, put out real and figurative fires, and find a way (at the cost of sleep) to get 'er done.

So, think back over these last few decades. What devastating situations or unexpected traumas have you brought your daughter or entire family through? And what character traits did you develop during those trying times? (Examples: ingenuity, creativity, perseverance, courage, grit, strength, sturdiness, faith, connection, fire, determination.)

Write them down. There's some real gold.

## Prompt 4: How has the "grinding wheel" sharpened you?

Do you remember way back when you were enjoying your six-year-old daughter and a mother of a teenager would burst your blissful bubble by saying, "Just you wait until she becomes a teen"? It always irritated me because I thought that mom was being so negative.

However...

In wisdom literature, there's a verse that goes, "As iron sharpens iron, so does one person sharpen another." Another translation is, "It takes a grinding wheel to sharpen a blade, and so one person sharpens the character of another."

I don't think it's a big reach for us moms to see how we've been the grinding wheel for our daughters—setting expectations, establishing boundaries, relentlessly monitoring. Allowing her to push against us to become the best version of herself. This is the tough and necessary work of parenting.

But friction abrades both sides, so it only makes sense that our daughters have sharpened us as well. I'd even argue there's no better grinding wheel than a teenage girl. They're hardwired to persistently push us moms to our limits. They don't back down, and they're always willing.

Most moms have experienced a season (or two) of unbearable, trying, hair-pulling times with their daughters. There are moments you think, *This is going to either destroy me or make me stronger.* And in those moments, you're not so sure which one it'll be.

Grinding wheel experiences can be anything that put you back on your heels or brought you to your knees. For instance,

- you found out your daughter sent a nude picture to her boyfriend and it got passed around school;

- your eighteen-year-old daughter told you she was pregnant;

- your daughter dyed her beautiful blonde hair black and got tatted up;

- your daughter told you she hates you;

- you discovered your daughter cutting herself;

- your daughter got a DUI;

- you found out that your daughter failed all her classes her first semester in college;

- your daughter got fired from her job because she overslept too many times.

Let me point out here that no matter the trauma, it only took your breath for a moment. Then, I'm guessing you went into mom-mode, figured out the next step, and helped your daughter move on from whatever impossible place she'd put herself. That's your gold.

Sometimes the grinding wheel is not a traumatic event but just the chronic arguing, disrespect, and entitlement. It's your daughter rehashing the details of her breakup six months later, or it's her constant drama. The repetition of these irritations day after day have a cumulative effect. I was talking to one of my friends about the grinding wheel, and she got it right away. She said, "I hear the grinding now and see those sparks flying."

When you're open, you can see that grinding wheel smoothing out the rough edges of your personality, shaping real and deep transformation. In my twenties I knew it all, and so I could be critical and judgmental. After the grinding wheel of parenting, my heart is so much bigger, my ego a lot smaller, and my compassion has expanded to moms all over the world.

I love what this mom said to me as she thought about her grinding wheel experiences: "I've been shattered in ways that I wouldn't have been without putting so much of my heart into the health and happiness of someone who is more vulnerable. And I've been more than restored after from the shattering over and over."

No mom puts a grinding wheel on her vision board. But because you're reading this book, I know those trying times didn't take you out. It would be lovely if we could all just attend a two-day retreat and have the same results—but there is no other way than through.

Now that these grinding wheel moments between you and your daughter are about to pass (for the most part), you have the emotional space to look back at what you've been through, how she challenged you, and how the friction of those challenges has shaped you and made you who you are today.

Think about it. And write it down.

## Prompt 5: What's been gained in the struggle?

Some of the hardest hard things are more ongoing struggles than traumatic events. Of course, such struggles change us. But the compassion, understanding, and practical knowledge you gain by living through them make you uniquely qualified to help others who experience the same.

Brandy's daughter Sophie struggled with severe depression and anger in high school. Then she was raped, further complicating her mental state. Sophie became extremely fragile and needed to be hospitalized. I walked with Brandy through this very difficult season of motherhood.

Though Brandy's heart was broken, she found it within herself to be there for Sophie as the mother Sophie needed. And Sophie healed. Over a long period of time and with her mother's love and support, Sophie was able to climb out of her dark abyss and get back on her feet. She graduated from college and is now living on her own.

As Brandy emerged from this struggle herself, she felt she had more to give. Her heart was big. She'd learned so much and now had a passion to help other girls suffering with similar trauma. Brandy got trained to counsel girls rescued from human trafficking. "Hearing their stories is hard," she says. "I know I make a difference. I know this is what I'm supposed to do." Brandy's heart and the skill to make that difference came from the greatest struggle she faced as a parent.

Meredith's daughter Leah had dyslexia and ADD. But that formal diagnosis wasn't made until Leah was in seventh grade, so all through Leah's grammar school years, Meredith had fought constantly with her—expressing frustration that Leah took forever with her homework, turned nothing in on time, and did poorly on tests.

Once Meredith realized the struggle her daughter had been going through all these years, she felt horrible guilt. She regretted the many times she lost her temper. But there was no time to wallow. Meredith apologized to Leah and then joined her daughter's struggle: Meredith secured support services for Leah at school. She did her own research to find out how to help her daughter manage her conditions. Meredith talked with psychiatrists, psychologists, and learning specialists to keep herself aware of the latest findings and techniques to help Leah. And with Meredith's consistent encouragement, understanding, and willingness to find a way, Leah flourished.

After Leah went to college, Meredith wanted to help other girls with learning differences—and their moms. She became a certified learning specialist and now has her own private practice.

Where have you faced struggles as a mom? What action did you take? What did you learn? What are you more aware of for having gone through it?

Write it down.

## Writing Your Second Draft

I hope you're realizing the mountain of ways in which you're better because of being a mom. All your experiences—the good and the hard—have given you more abilities, refined your character, and expanded your heart. And these mothering skills can absolutely transfer into other areas of your life, from volunteering to corporate, if you want.

But before you strike out on your own, let's get that second draft of your Mom Story committed to paper in a form that you can refer to as you need (and you're going to need to in the next several chapters).

Look at your notes from the prompts. You can write out a narrative or simply make a list, though I recommend the former. Take your time. There is no right or wrong way to do this. And this is for your eyes only—so don't worry about grammar or sentence structure or smooth transitions. Just start writing, and be sure to include

- the hats you've worn as a mom;
- the answer to how you did it;

- the interpersonal skills you've developed along the way;
- your abilities in handling the unexpected;
- how parenting has sharpened you, expanded you, and opened your heart;
- what you've gained through the struggles.

When you're finished, pour a glass of your favorite beverage. Sit somewhere comfortable with your second draft. Read it over slowly, savoring each sentence, each new skill, each accomplishment. Make a toast to all that gold. To all you've become through being a mother. To who you are today.

## This Second Draft Is So Important

Because...

- It's true.

- It debunks the big myth—that you haven't done any work or gained any marketable skills in the last twenty years.

- It frees you from any leftover mother shame or trauma.

- It helps you own all of your heroine's journey. You've traveled dark and treacherous terrain and have come through it loaded with gold.

- It gives you peace and contentment knowing that everything you did mattered.

- It gives you a humble and embodied confidence and knowledge.

- It expands your heart and compassion for others.

The second draft of your Mom Story is not final; it never is. But having worked through the second draft puts you in the right frame of mind to step into this next phase of your life. It puts you on the same forward trajectory with your daughter as you continue to be a positive role model for her by living fully and always evolving.

## Exercise: Give Yourself an Elevator Speech

PEOPLE INQUIRE all the time about our grown daughters. Sometimes it's fun to answer that question. "Oh, she just graduated from college and is headed to law school." And sometimes it's not so great. "Well, um, she's back home with us for a little while." Having a mom's elevator speech written and ready to go ensures you have a standard, go-to answer you feel good about.

The speech should be no more than a minute long—the time to travel from the first floor to the eighth in an elevator. You don't need a lot of details. But you want it to be the big story and be absolutely true. Look to your second draft to guide you in seeing that big story.

The elevator speech should work no matter what your daughter is up to. But it can be especially useful when your daughter is in a difficult season or you feel like the person asking is judging you.

I remember when an acquaintance said to me, "I just saw on social media that your daughter got another tattoo," I immediately felt judged as a bad mom and that my daughter had been deemed a bad daughter. I slipped right into a first-draft mentality, but then I remembered my elevator speech. "Yes, my daughter is incredibly creative," I replied. "I am so proud of how she's expressing her unique self. She continues to pursue her passions and is building an amazing business. She's an inspiration to me."

So, write yourself a little elevator speech—and then memorize it.

# 10

# Reconnecting to You

S I WRITE THIS, I'm visiting my good friend Sherry in Tucson (the same Sherry my daughter and I stayed with the night before my daughter headed out alone for a new life in Los Angeles). I'm staring out the window of the casita attached to Sherry's house and taking in the view of tall saguaro cacti against a deep blue sky. And it occurs to me, "She did it!"

Four years ago, when Sherry lived in Houston, we were taking a long walk around the Rice University campus. Her son was a senior in college then and about to graduate. Her daughter was a sophomore in college.

As we walked, Sherry told me she'd been struggling with asthma and allergies more than usual lately. I knew she'd been dealing with chronic bronchitis for years. She often joked she was allergic to everything—and East Texas's humid air wasn't helpful. So, it wasn't a huge surprise when she said she and her husband were thinking about moving to Tucson.

Tucson is where Sherry grew up. She still had family there—and lots of friends. Her parents were now in their eighties, and she wanted to enjoy these years with them. Also, Tucson is beautiful, and its climate is dry.

"Can you picture where you'd want to live in Tucson?" I asked.

Without missing a beat, she said, "We'd like to live in the foothills. My husband wants a mountain view. I want a casita next to the house where friends can stay."

"That sounds amazing and like you've already given it a lot of thought. What's keeping you from making the move?" I asked.

"It's a big ask for my husband," Sherry explained. "He would have to find another job. He'd be leaving his friends here. And you know I just opened the center." The Center for Postpartum Family Health—a professional milestone for Sherry. She continued, "I have six therapists working for me. My whole professional identity is in Houston. How can I manage the center if I don't live here? Not to mention, how could I leave the home I raised my kids in? Moving out of that house would be so painful, and what would my kids think? I'd be leaving our community. What if I do all of that, and I don't feel any better? How could I do that to my family? A big part of me feels obligated to stay in Houston."

Not long after that walk, Sherry got a staph infection in her sinuses. Her immune system was shot. The severity of her symptoms made her feel like remaining in Houston could shorten her life and a drier climate might be preferable—which her doctor confirmed. Her husband encouraged her to spend a month in Tucson to see if she'd do better there.

She did much better.

She realized she'd minimized how sick she'd been, especially in the last four years, and she couldn't ignore her health anymore. So, Sherry and her husband talked to the kids about moving to Arizona, and, to her surprise, they were more than supportive; they were excited about it. Her husband found out he could do his job remotely, which gave Sherry the idea that she could manage her center and her six therapists from Tucson. In the end, all those barriers she thought made a move to Tucson impossible crumbled pretty quickly when tested.

Once in Arizona, they found a terrific house with a pool in the backyard and a beautiful mountain view. It also had two garages, and right away Sherry saw one of them becoming a casita—the very one I'm sitting in as I write now.

Earlier today, Sherry and I walked in a saguaro forest in the hills and saw a pack of wild coyotes, a roadrunner, and a rabbit. We reminisced about our conversation at Rice University four years ago. She told me this move to Tucson had unequivocally been the right one for her health. She's found a great holistic doctor here, has been off all medications, and hasn't had bronchitis in two years. Also, her business in Houston is doing well. She has plans to expand and hire more therapists. Most important, though, she and her husband are happy here. She was so thankful to be able to support her parents during the Covid-19 pandemic. Her son and daughter love to come out to see them. And her aesthetically delightful casita has been filled with a steady stream of friends.

"Did you decorate your casita yourself?" I asked. "It's amazing."

"I did," she said. "Now that I don't have to take care of everyone, I have time to explore my creative side. I also put in the garden. And I'm playing around with music, photography, and painting again—all for the love of it."

She laughed at the resistance she'd felt toward this move and all those "reasons why not" she'd so quickly spouted off to me. "I was under some kind of 'mom spell' back then, denying myself to maintain some status quo for our family that nobody asked for or wanted. All it took was a brutal staph infection to make me see the light," she joked.

Here's the thing, as our offspring transition from dependent children to independent adults, what they need from us as parents changes. It's not serving them to preserve their childhood (including us) in amber. If what you want for your daughter is for her to seek out and live a rich and fulfilling life, to keep growing and learning, then you must model that. And that starts with reconnecting to you.

## What Does "Reconnecting to You" Mean, Anyway?

I know "reconnecting to you" can sound like one of those catchy subject lines on the cover of *O* magazine. But here's what I mean: When counseling moms, I'll say something like, "You should do something for yourself." Some look at me like a deer in the headlights. Others ask, "Like what? What would I do?" The majority have no idea what that something would be because it's been decades since they've even thought about what they like.

Of course, there was a time in your life when you not only did know what you liked but you also went after it with abandon. Then, around puberty, something changed for you—as it does for most female human beings. You stopped asserting yourself.

Since 1990, the American Association of University Women has annually polled boys and girls between the ages of nine and fifteen to ask about their attitudes toward self, school, family, and friends. Results consistently show that in those years, girls' confidence levels drop considerably.

How this confidence loss plays out in real life looks something like this: If you ask an eight-year-old girl what kind of pizza she wants, she'll say, "I want cheese pizza." If you ask the same girl two years later, she's likely to say something more like, "I don't care" or "What kind do you want?" Or worse, "It doesn't matter."

Why does this happen? Because girls are socialized to focus more on what others want. As puberty nears—and acceptance and relationships become more important—girls begin to defer their preferences to others in hopes of maintaining connections.

This dynamic—or management technique—only becomes more pronounced when we become moms. We focus on everyone else's needs and either put ours at the end of the never-ending to-do list or ignore them altogether. (Until our bodies start to scream at us, as Sherry's did.)

Moms try to keep everyone happy, to keep the peace, and to get the task done. When we poll the family about what to order for dinner or what movie to see or where to go on vacation, we honestly don't care what they choose, just as long as consensus is reached. Because what we really want is one thing less on the list. The problem is, after decades of disregarding them, we forget what our preferences are. We lose our connection to our innermost thoughts, feelings, preferences, and desires.

I had a mom in my office who was planning a huge family trip to the tropics, sailing to multiple islands. When I asked her what part of the trip she was looking forward to the most, she couldn't think of anything. I mean ... that's sad. She was that disconnected from herself.

## Clear Away the Obstacles to You

So, now the task becomes to reconnect—to get you back in touch with all those things that make you *you*. How hard can that be? Life has calmed down, right? There's no longer a kitchen table full of people with demands on your time. It's just you—and your partner, if you have one. Surely, nothing is preventing you from focusing on yourself.

While that may be the objective truth, it's likely not your current lived reality. Because while your daughter has moved out of the house, parenting and the mind games that come with it probably have yet to move out of your head. Two of the biggest parenting mind games— false obligations and false comparisons—are also two of the biggest barriers to reconnection.

Let's start with *false obligations*. An obligation is the condition of being morally or legally bound to do something. But *feeling like* you owe somebody—your kids, your husband, your best friend, your community—something doesn't mean you do. If the tie is emotion alone, it's a false obligation.

What's a little tricky here for moms of newly independent daughters is that what used to be true obligations—maintaining a stable home for her or considering her immediate needs when making your life choices—are now false obligations. And the danger with false obligations is they keep you from acting on what's real for you now.

Sherry, like so many of us moms do, felt obligated to stay in the house her children grew up in. She felt obligated not to ask her husband to move to Tucson. Both false obligations that kept her stuck and physically ill in Houston. If you feel obligated to stay in a house or in a job or even with a hairdresser you don't like, you give yourself no choice but to stay. However, when you free yourself from false obligations, you free yourself to consider what you do want and what's best for you (and probably for everyone)—just as Sherry did for herself and her family. Feeling trapped is a big clue you're limiting yourself because of a false obligation.

Like false obligations, *false comparisons* get in the way of you knowing yourself. As parents, we can't help but look outside ourselves for guidance, see what other moms are doing—especially in times of transition. After all, there's never been a manual to tell us how this parenting thing is done. Typically, though, before we pick up any helpful hints, we've already started comparing ourselves to other moms.

Instagram and Facebook are breeding grounds for such false comparisons. You see the mom on social media who's in perfect shape, with perfect children, a loving husband, and an amazing side hustle. You can't help but feel less than, which never feels good. You discount yourself as the has-been, geeky mom—not important, nothing special, and looks like a loser.

If you could only pull your sights back a little, you'd see that you're comparing your living, breathing self to a two-dimensional image. What looks perfect from your vantage, might look very different when standing in her shoes. You have no idea what's really going on in her life, or in anyone else's, so your comparison is a false comparison.

But really, all comparisons are false. You can't compare two lives any more than you can compare two children. You are unique, your relationship to your daughter is unique, your life is unique. And what's unique, by definition, has no comparison.

## Put Your Attention Back on You

Let's call out your false obligations, ditch the false comparisons, and put your focus where it should be: on you. Reconnecting to you is not about looking around you, anyway. It's about looking inside of you. Which can be scary. Especially if you haven't done it in a while.

Many of my clients are afraid that if they look too closely at themselves, they'll find they don't matter or there's nothing special about them. I ask them if they'd have those concerns if we were talking about their daughter—or any other human being. "Of course not," they always say. To which I reply, "Then why would that be true of you?" I mean this: you are a miracle, your authenticity is beautiful, and your heart matters.

There are parts of ourselves we've forgotten on this journey of motherhood. It's time to reclaim them, which is not only doable but easier than you think. As with most things, reconnecting to yourself comes down to giving it your attention.

One of the most valuable commodities you have is your attention. The problem is that everyone and everything is vying for it all the time—but at no time more than in your parenting years. When your daughter was small, your attention was splattered everywhere—tending to her, keeping your home running, working, and a million other things. As your daughter entered her teens, trying and traumatic circumstances took your attention. So, spending your attention on yourself during those years felt frivolous—it was a habit you let go of.

But that was then, Mom. This is now. And now it's time to get back in the habit of putting your attention on yourself. Here are two steps to help you reinstate this focus:

## Step 1: Pay Attention to Your Preferences

I just got back from getting my eyes checked. To make sure I have the right lens prescription, the optometrist showed me one image and then another. She then asked, "Which is better?" I had to make a decision and tell her.

Paying attention to your preferences starts with remembering to ask yourself, which is better? The key here is to show yourself you have an opinion and recognize it matters. I couldn't tell my optometrist, "It doesn't matter." Because it did.

Begin with the little stuff. What kind of music do you like? What shows do you like to watch? What's your favorite movie? Your favorite pizza toppings? What sheets do you like? What flowers make you happiest? What would your perfect day be? What's your favorite dessert or smoothie?

Next, say your preferences out loud to another human. Even better, order the pizza, the sheets, or the flowers you like, and enjoy them.

And finally, to complete this first step of "paying attention to your preferences," get in the practice of not deferring to others. This takes more courage, but it actually makes you a more interesting person, and it's really not that hard to do. For instance, the next time someone asks where you'd like to have dinner, tell them. You're not insisting, you're simply making your preference part of the decision equation—as it should be. See how it feels.

Rebuilding your preference muscle can bring you so much joy. With every choice, you'll find yourself happier and more satisfied. And it's totally within your reach.

## Step 2: Pay Attention to Your Feelings

Another basic conduit to self-connection that gets lost in the throes of parenting is recognizing our feelings. When we're full throttle in the motherhood grind, we're just trying to get through the day. Feelings become a nuisance, a hindrance to productivity. The only feelings that can get through are those that alert us to danger—like fear, anxiety, stress, and frustration. When that's all we allow ourselves to feel, however, having feelings becomes uncomfortable. The next thing we know, we're trying to outrun or numb them.

But when you numb the difficult feelings, the feel-good feelings get numbed too. Decades of this can leave us like the Tin Man in *The Wizard of Oz*, thinking we're without a heart. We need our feelings to point us toward what we desire, what's important to us. Without a heart, unable to feel our emotions, we lose the sacred guidance they provide.

To reawaken your heart and give your feelings the attention they've been missing, get in the habit of asking yourself how you feel after interactions with others. For instance, after a conversation with your partner, employee, daughter, or ex-husband, give yourself space to take note of what you're feeling and glean any wisdom from that feeling that it might hold for you.

Don't take the first emotion you feel at face value. Feelings can be layered. Underneath anger is often fear. Underneath judgment can be shame. Difficult feelings can dominate and squelch feelings like love. You did a lot of work on your feelings in the first and second drafts of your Mom Story, especially around disappointment and resentment. Remember how both of those negative feelings drew your attention to what was missing in your life and what you wanted more of. Emotions can be messy. It takes presence and space to get clear. Sometimes a professional guide can be a great help in this process.

As you sort through the old stuff, the hard stuff, the confusing stuff, be sure you open your heart to the new stuff, the easy stuff, the good-feeling stuff. Pay attention to the little things around you that bring you delight, that lift your spirit. Sometimes they appear in subtle ways like a bud on a barren branch in spring, a beautiful waterfall, or aspen leaves fluttering in the wind. Sometimes it's a feeling of gratitude for time together with family or good friends.

A great tool for staying current with your emotions is journaling. Ask yourself two questions: What am I feeling? And, What can I learn from my feelings? And then write freely for twenty minutes. Don't edit. Don't judge. Just name all the feelings that come up and why. You can take this even further by asking, What can I learn from my feelings? What are they asking me to do? This easy practice will give you important insights and strengthen your reconnection to yourself.

## Recognize What You've Outgrown

Also evidenced by your Mom Story drafts (especially the second draft), you haven't stopped growing as a person. But as you've grown, you've also outgrown, so as you "reconnect to you," take inventory. Decide what in your life no longer fits and what might better suit who you are and what you want for yourself now. You can start by looking at your house, your relationships, and your work and asking what needs to be changed, remodeled, or rebuilt.

## House: What Have You Outgrown?

Many moms start to remodel their home when their daughter leaves for college. It can be very therapeutic to declutter and get rid of old toys, clothes, and your daughter's stick figure drawings, macaroni art, and other preschool projects.

I, however, was not one of those moms. It took repeated observations by my nearly adult daughter to open my eyes: "Mom, oh my gosh, how long are you going to have my Beanie Babies on your bookshelf?" And, "Your room has been painted yellow for how many years? When are you going to change that?" And, "You do realize you have no *current* pictures of me or you or us in this house... ?"

Yikes, she was right on every count. I was so used to living in my house I didn't see how stuck in the past I was. But after she pointed it out, I couldn't un-see it. This started me on a very self-affirming project that readied my house and me for this new phase in my life; it's a project I recommend to the majority of my clients, and now to you.

Look around your home and use these questions to reflect:

1 Are there things you can let go of? (Old Barbies, T-shirts from college, CDs?)

2 Do you like the color of your walls and trim?

3 Is there any part of your space you want to reclaim?

4 How about some deep purging in your daughter's bedroom, closet, or bathroom?

5 Do you like your furniture, your mattress, your dishes, your decorations?

Whatever you've outgrown or don't like anymore, change. Use your newly rediscovered preferences to guide you.

## Relationships: What Needs to Change?

Take an honest look at the relationships (friendships, family, partners) in your life. For each, ask: Does this relationship energize me or leave me feeling anxious or drained? Do I feel seen or dismissed? Does this relationship support my growth or bring out my worst? Does it have a natural give and take, or do I do all the giving? Does it bring me joy or heaviness?

You want relationships with people who see you and accept you for everything you are. Such relationships are worth pure gold. They provide love and support whether you're a mess or a superstar. They keep you connected to yourself.

You also want relationships with people who are committed to their own growth and so naturally support yours. I found these types of friends when I hired a coach and joined a small mastermind group of women entrepreneurs. Many of these like-minded women have become cherished friends and consistently give me invaluable encouragement.

But some relationships aren't so good for you, so it's time to decide which of those to sever completely and which to keep (but at a distance). These are people—friends or family members—you feel stifled around. Usually that's because they aren't interested in developing themselves and so don't like it much when your life expands. A good litmus test when deciding if a relationship is toxic for you is answering the question, "Do I feel more myself when I'm with them or away from them?"

At this point, you may be thinking, *The biggest energy drain in my life is my husband (or partner).* You wouldn't be alone. I'd say that's a phrase I hear quite often in my practice. However, sorting through the complexities of such a major relationship is a whole other book.

That said, let me give you a few things to think about here. Parenting takes a toll, not only on you but also on the marriage. When your kids move out and the dust settles, issues that were never dealt with during the demanding parenting years rise to the surface. You may feel you've outgrown your marriage. Maybe you have. But maybe you just need to rebuild it some. Well-known speaker Beth Moore often says, "I've had seven different marriages with the same man." Marriage therapy might be the right answer here. While that can be hard work, it can also deepen your connection to yourself and your spouse. Because now you'll be bringing your thoughts, your feelings, and your preferences into this upgraded version of your marriage.

## Work: Is Your Work Working for You?

First, let me say that all moms work, even if they are stay-at-home moms. But whether or not you work outside the home, once the kids are gone, you have more freedom, so it's a great time to evaluate your volunteer work or your career.

I've talked to so many moms who feel pressure and heaviness around work—either having a job or not having one. Some returned to work to help pay their daughter's tuition. But when their daughter graduates from college, they aren't sure if they should quit or if they will even want to. Some moms want to reenter the workforce but are scared because they don't know how. Still others are tired of the same volunteer job they've held for years, but they are afraid if they leave, no one can replace them.

Even if you love what you do, this can be a great time to tweak how you work. Let's put the pressure aside and have some fun here. Again, we want you to reconnect to yourself and your preferences. Get out your journal and commit to writing on this topic for thirty minutes using these prompts:

### Prompt 1: Start with where you are now.
Name how you feel about work (paid or volunteer) and where you feel ambivalent. For instance, maybe you like where you work, but you can't stand your boss. Or you like what you do, but you work too many hours. Maybe you're bored and want a challenge. Or you hate the corporate politics and want to call your own shots. Do you love it? Or do you feel stuck? Are you being held captive by false obligations?

## Prompt 2: Dream a little.

Now that you're no longer limited by school hours or going to your kid's games and performances, let's dream a little. What does your ideal work look like? Use the following questions to help you visualize the ultimate work situation for you: Would you work at home? Do you like the energy of an office with coworkers? Would you travel, and how often? Are you ready to leave corporate and start your own business? Would you like to create a new product, write a book, or start selling your paintings? Or do you want to leave your stressful accounting job and work in a cute retail store?

The good news is you're not stuck; you have choices! At home, in your relationships, at work—you don't need to make drastic changes now (though you can). You just need to give some attention to yourself, decide what and who can support you best in doing that, and create a life environment that keeps your connection to yourself open and flowing.

## Reconnect to Your Deeper Self

If parenthood has taught us nothing else, it's that we know more than we think we do and we're more capable than we ever imagined. You have a wealth of resources inside you that, when listened to, steer you in the right direction even when—especially when—you don't know how or why. Some call it a sixth sense, an inner wisdom, a gut feeling, a deep knowing. Some call it mother's intuition.

As a mother, you know when "something's not right" with your child. You can feel when your daughter's not okay, even if she's miles away. More than once this feeling has likely caused you to reach out with a text or call. And yes, sometimes you've been accused of being a drama mama. But more often than not, your intuition was spot-on: she needed you.

You also know when "something has to change" with your child. How many times as a mom have you spent a million hours ruminating about a situation and then in a flash the notion that something must change comes to you and you act. Like when you pulled your daughter out of the gifted math program in third grade, against all advice. But you could feel how miserable she was, how boring the teacher was, and you knew somehow that if you allowed this situation to continue out of some sense of false pride, your daughter might hate math forever, squashing her actual gift for numbers.

And, Mom, you *know* when "something is just right." Sometimes it doesn't even make sense, but you know it. Like when your brilliant daughter decided not to go to college but to go to work after high school. Even though that wasn't your dream for her, you supported her because it felt right. Now, five years on, she has people working for her and is taking the college classes she feels she needs as she prepares to open her own business.

I think our deep knowing is there throughout our lives. Parenthood just makes it more pronounced... and necessary. But now that you know you have it and know how to access it, you can redirect it and use its wisdom to strengthen your connection to yourself. This inner guide can become your guide to what is true for you, what you long for, what you desire, and what you want to do.

But first you have to make space for it. You have to get quiet so you can hear your inner voice. Silence, meditation, prayer, yoga, and journaling can all help you clear that space that your body needs to relax so you can take full advantage of your deeper self for yourself.

## Reconnect to Your Curiosity

In her article "What to Do If You *Can't* Find Your Passion," published on Oprah.com, Elizabeth Gilbert writes, "If you've lost your life's true passion (or if you're struggling desperately to find passion in the first place), don't sweat it. Back off for a while. But don't go idle, either. Just try something different, something you don't care about so much. Why not try following mere curiosity, with its humble, roundabout magic?"

When I have a client who's overwhelmed by the idea of reconnecting to themselves, I have them try going in using the back door of curiosity. Curiosity is accessible to all of us. It gently calls us to take one baby step out of our predictable and known life by simply asking questions—nothing more.

- Could I make vegan chocolate chip cookies?
- Could I grow tomatoes in my backyard?
- What would it take to start a blog?
- What would my hair look like with waves?
- What would it take to create an online course?
- What does it take to be a good speaker?
- I have an idea for a business—what would happen if I worked with a few clients?

When you move your curiosity muscle every day, your questions naturally reveal what's uniquely interesting to you—which reveals you. It doesn't matter if you're curious about things others find insignificant. Curiosity wakes you from the doldrums of a routine life. It's the secret sauce that moves you forward. Sherry's curiosity led her to her creative side. Which led to her dabbling with watercolors, playing guitar, learning how to garden in the desert, and, of course, decorating her casita.

As you move forward into this new phase of parenting and life, whenever you feel yourself overwhelmed and disconnecting, let your curiosity bring you back to yourself.

## Mom, Know Thyself

My hope is that first and foremost you reconnect to yourself so you can realize all you are and share the fullness of you with the world. But also, be aware that as your daughter takes her first tenuous steps into independent adulthood, she's looking back to you to see how it's done. When she turns her head, what do you want her to see: A woman clinging to a past that's gone, tethered by false obligation, and burdened by false comparisons? Or someone who's plugged into her wisdom, who's curious, and who's continuing to grow? Someone who pays attention to herself, who has preferences and makes them known. Someone who cares for herself, as she cares for those she loves. You, Mom, are the trailblazer for your daughter. Live the life you want her to follow.

## Exercise: Time to Take Action

NOW THAT you've paid attention to these different facets of yourself, it's time to take action. This chapter covered four opportunities for reconnection:

- identifying your preferences
- updating your home, relationships, and/or work
- tapping into your intuition
- getting curious

My very easy challenge: I would like you to do one thing from each category.

- Pick a preference and act on it.

- Update one thing at home, in a relationship, or at work.

- Quiet your mind in whatever way you prefer and give your deeper wisdom some space.

- Get curious about something and see where the rabbit hole leads.

I'm only asking you to do one thing because I want to make this so easy you have no excuses. I also want you to see how good it feels to reconnect to you. You can make it simple (preferences: buy your favorite Ben & Jerry's ice cream) or challenging (relationships: have a healing conversation with your sister). Whichever inspires you to take action.

# 11

# Dial Up Your Dream

N 2009, I'd been a therapist for fifteen years and felt a little cramped in my therapist cave. I still liked seeing clients, but I wanted to do more and have a bigger reach. I had no idea what that was or how to do it. I knew I couldn't do it alone. I needed a mentor or guide and support from other like-minded women. So, after some research, I joined my first yearlong mastermind, led by business coach Christine Kane.

Our second two-day retreat was in Tucson. It was my first time experiencing the beauty of the desert. (This was a decade before Sherry moved there.) Twelve of us stayed at a lovely resort at the base of the Catalina Foothills.

I woke up the first day eager for what it would bring, especially to see how our amazing coach would wield her magic. I walked past swimming pools, cacti, and palm trees to get to our meeting room. We all sat around a long table. In turn, each woman stood in the front of the room, where Christine would ask her what she wanted in her career or life and then encourage her to commit to a few specific actions that would move her toward realizing that aspiration.

That's when each woman started crawfishing (Southern slang for retreating). There came the excuses, the limiting beliefs, the self-doubt, and stories of why it wasn't possible. Christine didn't buy our small stories of ourselves. She told us it was her responsibility to hold us to our highest and best selves. I watched as she, like a skilled surgeon, cut through our resistance and, quite frankly, our BS too. Her superpower was seeing our bigness, our light, our potential, and holding space for that. By the time we finished up, I still hadn't faced the "question." It would be my turn the next day. But even though it had been powerful to watch Christine work with the others, I was terrified of being that exposed and vulnerable. Honestly, I was dreading it.

That evening after dinner, my new comrades and I hung out in the hotel lobby. These were my kind of women—a fun group. After about two glasses of wine, our humor spun out of control. We acted like teenagers. We respected and feared Christine. We joked about her intensity. And then as she walked through the lobby, we thought we'd share our "humor" with her. Christine didn't say anything; she just walked off. We kind of felt bad but sloughed it off.

Our "humor" was really sarcasm, which is basically fear veiled in anger. We made fun of what we were afraid of. We were afraid of looking foolish, of being judged. We were afraid that we couldn't do it. It felt risky, scary, and uncomfortable all at the same time. We were caught in this internal tug of war between wanting more and feeling we didn't deserve it.

The next day after breakfast, I walked to our meeting room. On the door was one of those gigantic sticky notes with a message in colorful markers. This sticky note changed the direction of my life.

Here's what it said:

**YOU ARE ENTERING THE OFFICIAL PLAY BIG ZONE.**

*The following is prohibited:*
sarcasm, whining, complaining,
blaming anyone or anything about your results,
distracting or self-deprecating humor,
being a victim.

*The following is required:*
Taking full responsibility for your life and your results,
claiming the powerful woman you are,

recognizing that your clarity makes you unstoppable,
deciding to live from your clearest, highest, whole self,
becoming the person you are destined to be,
full engagement, no checking out.

This is not a joke. Take one moment. Get still inside. Be clear.
Be powerful—then, and only then,
step inside...

Several of us gathered by the door. We stood there reading in dead silence. At first, I felt like the teenage girl who just got busted. Then I thought, *What if Christine sees something in me that I can't see yet? I don't think of myself as a powerful woman. What would it even look like if I lived from my clearest, highest, whole self?*

Despite my doubt, I felt this flicker of hope in my heart. I realized Christine was holding me accountable to something terrifying yet exhilarating at the same time. She was holding me accountable to my light, my destiny, and my bigness. I made a decision that day to grow up and take responsibility for my life. Yes, I was crazy scared to enter the Play Big Zone. But I took a deep breath and walked inside.

Looking back now, half the people in that first mastermind retreat group disregarded the message, and their lives have stayed the same. I see some of their posts on Facebook, complaining about the same things they complained about a decade ago.

The other half took this message seriously, and we've become the best of friends. Over the years, we've stood shoulder to shoulder, cheering each other on as we continue to take risks and move forward. It feels miraculous how I've changed and what I've created since 2009, and I can trace it all back to that one moment I decided to play big.

## Taking a Cue from Our Daughters

Your daughter is in the midst of playing big right now herself, dialing up her dream. You've watched her from up close as she's moved toward a life defined by her passions and desires. And as you've witnessed, it didn't happen in one magical moment with angels singing. It's been a messy, exciting, grueling, rewarding, up-and-down journey.

Maybe your daughter rode her horse every day and competed in shows since middle school in her pursuit to get on a college equestrian team. Perhaps she trained several hours a day throughout high school and attended summer internships to get a scholarship for dance. Or maybe your more introverted daughter built a portfolio and got accepted to the School of the Art Institute of Chicago to study fashion design.

It doesn't matter if your daughter was outgoing or introverted, dead set on a direction or didn't have a clue; it took courage for her to move out into the world after high school without a guaranteed outcome. It took courage to leave her home, family, and friends and create a whole new set of relationships and community. It took courage to leave what she knew—to leave what's comfortable. In other words, it took courage to take a risk.

But your daughter pushed through her fear, mucked through all her uncertainty and wishy-washiness, and committed to going for it. You continue to expect and will accept nothing less of her.

So, now it's your turn, Mom. And you should expect and accept nothing less of yourself. Your daughter is working toward realizing her own dream, so she can't be your dream anymore. It's time you put your focus back on you and what you want out of life. It's time to dial up a dream of *your* own. (Luckily, if you need instructions or inspiration, you need look no further than your own daughter.)

## Reclaiming Your Dial

When our daughters are eighteen, we don't fully grasp what their leaving home really means for us. But by the time they're in their twenties, they have their own lives. And if we've done our job as mothers well, their dreams don't feature us. We'll always have a supporting role in their lives, but we're no longer a lead. (Though I know this is a developmentally good thing, I don't like hearing it any better than you. Yet, it's true.)

When the time comes, it's tempting to kid ourselves that our daughters haven't really gone away, to pretend they're on a long vacation and will come home again. But your daughter's intent now isn't to come back home. You're no longer an active, day-in, day-out parent. Now that she's on her way to taking full control of her dial, it's time for you to reclaim yours. It's time for you to retake the central role in your own life story.

You've done lots of brave things as a mother—found strength and capabilities you didn't know you had. Now you need to gather that strength for yourself... as well as for her. Remember that taking the leap and turning the dial a little more not only moves you closer to living a fulfilling life, it also puts you on a parallel path with your daughter, allowing you to be a real support to her. This new phase—any new phase—is scary and exciting. We won't always know what we're doing. Our daughters won't either. By moving forward in our own lives, we show them how to face and manage through the uncertainty, and how to be resilient.

## Where to Begin

When I ask the question, "What do you want to do with your life?" what feelings come up for you? Anger, sadness, excitement, hope, fear? Often it's a cluster of feelings, with a heaping helping of uncertainty.

Maybe, like me in 2009 before I entered the Play Big Zone, you have no idea exactly what your dream is or how to get there. Maybe you have just a glimmer of hope that there's something more for you. That's fine. Because that's all it takes to get started.

You don't have to know everything right now. This is your life and your dream. You get to define it. You get to determine its size. You get to move your dial at your own pace—one click at a time, if you like.

"Dialing up your dream" or "playing big" doesn't mean becoming famous or making a million dollars. This isn't about being Melinda Gates, Brené Brown, or Oprah Winfrey. This is about being you. It's about finding something that captures your attention and your heart. A pursuit that helps you contribute from your unique talents, gifts, and experience. Maybe even the inkling of a calling that allows you to make a difference in the world, in your own way.

You may be thinking that all sounds well and good, but you still don't have the foggiest idea what that something is for you. I can't tell you how many times in my practice I hear, "I don't know what I want." What my clients usually mean is they can't see the end goal. But Mom, you don't have to know the end. You just need to know where you want to begin.

In truth, you've already started dialing up your dream as you've read this book. In the previous two chapters, you reconnected to yourself and acknowledged your many talents and strengths. You started paying attention to your preferences, following your curiosity, and taking a hard look at what (and who) you want to stay in your life and what (and who) needs to go. My guess is you've already moved your dial by cleaning out a closet or two, getting rid of some frumpy clothes, or signing up for a yoga class. Click by click, you've been moving closer to a life that reflects you. So, let's build on that momentum.

Now it's time to move with *intention* toward your dream. To take stock of what you love and do that. Lots of moms tell me that once their nest is empty, they'll "just" work in a boutique to keep themselves busy. That's a place to start, to be sure. You get a few clicks on the dial for trying something new and playing a role other than mom. And if retail is what you love, great. But if not, if you chose this by default, just because it's something you thought you "could" do, I encourage you to keep an open mind and explore different directions for yourself. Notice, I did not say destination. All you are looking for right now is what feels good to you, what feels right, what's worth a follow-up, maybe even dipping your toe in and trying.

So, toss all the demands in your life out of your head. Your direction will not be defined by what your husband or daughter or mother want for you. Or by money woes. This isn't about getting a job—though that might be an outcome. It's not about false obligations or shoulds—like you should be available 24/7 to take your mom or dad to medical appointments, or you should do the bookkeeping for your husband's business. Even if you have to do some of those things, you don't want them to be all that fills your days.

When you are ready, ask yourself these two questions:

## Question 1: What would a dream life look like?

Once your mind is clear, begin to fill it back up by creating a beautiful picture of your dream life. Make it vivid. Fill in the details. What is the most stunning, fulfilling, joyous, exciting, and meaningful life you can imagine for yourself? When you can see that life, journal about it. Then ask yourself what baby step you might take to move you toward it. And there's your direction. For instance, if you saw yourself in Paris painting and packing your brushes and booking a ticket to France isn't in the budget right now, maybe sign up for a local art class instead. Click.

## Question 2: Where do I want to give back?

The real reason I was able to step inside that door and play big in 2009 was I got over myself and didn't make it about me. My ego and my insecurities could have stopped me dead in my tracks. You know: "Who am I to do this?" "How dare I?" But when I switched the questions to: How can I serve? How can I help? How can I make a difference? How can I give back?, this is what got me through the door. I invite you to think about what you want through this lens: What do you want to give back?

As moms, we have proven ourselves to be highly relational. We are nurturing, empathic, caring, and fiercely protective of those we love. The world—and our communities—desperately need our highly developed instincts and resourcefulness. Imagine if every mother took on the challenges of her community with the same ingenuity and energy she brought to mothering—we would literally change our planet for good. So, ask yourself: What breaks your heart? What pulls on your heartstrings? Where do you know you can help? What fulfills you? What rocks your world? Where do you want to direct all that nurturing that so far you've been giving primarily to your daughter? And there's your direction.

Whatever comes to you doesn't have to be your full-time job or your complete "dream"—though it could be. Right after her kids left home, my friend Sherry volunteered at her church helping refugees. She said it felt good to be of use and help others as she found her way to what was next for her.

## If Your Dial Still Feels Stuck

If you're still feeling unsure, like it's all moving too fast, that's okay. Big changes in our routines, especially when they involve our identity, are never easy. Change itself is never easy. Yet it comes, and our only choice is how to deal with it, how we use it.

Luckily, we can learn from the experience of mothers who reached this stage before us. In my practice, here are the most common things I see that keep the dream dial stuck (several of which I've experienced myself):

### Fear We'll Lose Our Daughters

My daughter is in a very committed relationship, and I think they'll get married. On my good days, I couldn't be happier. But she's not as available as she used to be. Yesterday (a bad day), I was talking to her and she canceled our plans to get together because of work and her boyfriend. At that moment, I missed her so much I would've thrown my new life out the window to get back to the good old days when I could see her more frequently. I let her know how disappointed I was.

Needless to say, this was an overreaction. (By the way, she just wanted to push our plans back one week!) My limbic button got pressed. I felt like I was losing her. Later I texted my daughter and apologized for getting ruffled; she graciously accepted. Thank God for my full life or *I* would drive *my daughter* crazy.

When our daughters leave, there is a void in our lives emotionally and in our days practically, even for women who already had busy careers while raising kids. If we don't fill those voids with our own interests, our neediness is likely to suffocate our daughters—and iron-ically, we'll lose them. They'll distance themselves from us for their own survival.

A mom in her sixties and her two forty-something daughters (both with families of their own) made an appointment with me to work on their relationships. The mother felt completely rejected by her daughters and wanted more time with her grandchildren.

Mom expressed she was angry and hurt that her daughters wouldn't go to lunch with her every week. With that declaration, the older daughter became furious and called her mom selfish. The truth was the daughter was raising four children. She barely had time to take a shower, let alone go to lunch. Still, the mother had succeeded in making both daughters feel guilty for this. Not exactly the mother-daughter relationship any of us aspires to.

You can't find your dream solely in your children's or grandchildren's lives. It's not fair to them. And it is not fair to you either. Our adult daughters have moved on and, if we are to have a meaningful relationship with them, we need to move on with our lives too.

## Low-to-No Expectations for What's Possible

Perhaps you think it's all fine and good for your daughter to go for it, but your glory days have passed; your future was yesterday. You think if something hasn't happened yet in your life, it's not going to happen. One client told me she didn't know any fifty-year-old women who were happy at work. They all thought their best days were behind them.

In his book *Brainstorm*, Dr. Daniel Siegel proposes that we older adults need to re-awaken the "gift" of adolescence to maintain our vitality. As he explains, "This is the essence of living well during adolescence and during the adult years: *Emotional Spark—Social Engagement—Novelty—Creative Explorations.*" (You can remember them by using the acronym ESSENCE.) Dr. Siegel encourages us to bring that adol-ESSENCE to our adult-ESSENCE. "Adolescents can remind us of what we have a right to experience in our lives," he writes.

You, Mom, have the right to have an emotional spark, like feeling delight, pleasure, and love. You have the right to broaden and deepen your social connections. You have a right to experience new things, learn new skills, and travel and encounter different cultures if you want. You have a right to have creative exploration and see the world through new lenses.

Encouraging your adult-ESSENCE is good for your brain, your health, and the relationships in your life—including the one with your daughter. ESSENCE isn't reserved for the young. And all of us—including you—have the ability to cultivate it.

The expectations you set for your life now are up to you.

## Lost Hope

A companion obstacle to low expectations is lost hope. At some point, you decided your dreams couldn't be realized, that they weren't possible. Sometimes this is caused by a trauma knocking the wind—and hope—out of us. But it can also happen because life just takes over. It takes everything we have to get by—a slower trauma of sorts. So, our dreams are put on hold until, unconsciously, we decide they just aren't attainable in this lifetime. Our hearts go numb. And we lose hope.

- You got divorced and wanted to marry again. When it didn't happen, it hurt less not to hope.

- You wanted to write a book. But between work and kids, after a while, it seemed pointless.

- You wanted to start your own business. But you couldn't justify the financial risk, so you filed it under "unrealistic."

- You wanted to start a nonprofit to help young mothers in Africa. But everyone said it was ridiculous, so you stopped thinking about it.

- You were hoping to live in a beautiful home with a view. But the house you have is fine and paid for, so you shut that dream down.

- You always wanted to travel to Italy or Greece. But it would be expensive. You'd never have the budget, so why entertain the thought?

- You wanted to be in better shape and be more active. But what else is new? Your efforts have never worked before, so why would they work now?

- You wanted to have a better relationship with your daughter. *But she has her own life now, so you stopped trying.*

I'd like to challenge you here. How do you know what's possible and what's not? You don't. None of us knows what our future holds. What if you *can* have what you wanted? You don't have to make a strategic plan. Just open yourself to the possibility that what you hope for in the deepest part of your heart is possible. That maybe now is the time for that dream. That your best days are ahead of you.

## General Fear

Underlying all these obstacles is the biggest obstacle of all—general fear. Gollum's voice once again taunts and intimidates us, so we don't dare to dream.

- When you think about getting married again, fear chimes in: *Who'd marry you anyway? If you did marry again, it might be worse than the first time.*

- As you contemplate finally writing that book, fear tells you: *You don't know how to write. No one would buy your book. Who do you think you are?*

- When you dream of starting your own business, fear pops in to say: *What if it fails? What if you go bankrupt? What if you can't pay your bills? What if you hate it?*

- As you reconsider your dream to have a nonprofit to help young mothers in Africa, fear laughs: *You have no idea how to make this work. You'd be overwhelmed.*

- When you rekindle your desire to have a beautiful home with a view, fear chides: *You should be content with what you have. You can't afford it anyway.*

- As you daydream about that trip to Italy or Greece, fear reminds: *That's so far away. You don't speak the language. And something bad could happen while you're gone.*

- As you consider joining a gym to get in better shape and be more active, fear says: *You can't win. You'll gain back any weight lost, and you're just too out of shape anyway.*

- Right when you think it's possible to have a better relationship with your daughter, fear whispers: *She's finally rid of you. Why would she want to work on your relationship now?*

Embedded in all these thoughts is the fear of failing, fear of rejection, fear of not being in control, fear of being hurt, fear of being disappointed, fear of something new, fear of putting yourself out there and looking a fool, and, of course, there are always money fears.

In 2009, I was hit hard with many of those same fears. But I walked through that door at the mastermind. And over the next twelve years, I just kept turning up the dial one click at a time. Now, two books, a popular TEDx talk, and a successful podcast later, I have helped more moms from around the world than I could have ever imagined.

Maybe you're thinking, *Sure, but that's you. I couldn't possibly...*

Well, I didn't think I could possibly either. But I learned to deal with the fear by leaning into it. Now "feel the fear" is my motto. Whenever I'm faced with a challenge or an opportunity that scares me, I walk myself through this process:

1  I feel the fear.

2  I see if there is a practical message in it. (For instance: You need some training before you do a radio show.)

3  If there is something practical I can do, I do it.

4  If there's no practical message, I continue to feel my fear and go for what I want anyway.

As moms, we need to be aware of an extra sneaky way we have of skirting fear and not entering the Play Big Zone. In our active parenting years, when we were afraid of putting ourselves out there, trying something new, or showing up fully, many of us hid behind our children. This not only got us out of fear-inducing situations, it made us look like self-sacrificing angels at the same time. For instance, maybe we turned down an opportunity to speak at a conference because we told ourselves and everyone else we didn't travel because we had kids at home. But the truth was we were scared to speak in public. Or we gave up painting because we said our children needed our attention. But the truth was we were scared our talent had reached its peak long ago. Or we declined an invitation to join a bowling league, saying we needed to be home at night for our daughters. But the truth was we felt awkward around new people.

If you've used this tactic to sidestep opportunities for your growth (and who among us has not), then be prepared. Because once your daughter is gone, your cover will be gone too. You and your fears will no longer have anywhere to hide.

This doesn't have to be a bad thing. It's an invitation to show up for your life. To *feel the fear*. To mine it for insight. To let it speak to you if it has something to say. To step over the obstacle and move toward what's calling you.

## Being Too Comfortable

I'm not down on comfort; I love being comfortable. I have a refrigerator magnet with a woman lying in a plush bed with the caption, "I love not camping." Why? I like to be comfortable. But I do think we can get *too* comfortable.

Sheila was married and had been a stay-at-home mom. Her daughter had required a lot of attention in high school but now was twenty-three and in law school, living on her own. With her daughter gone, Sheila felt bored. Though she had a list of chores (from her husband), she ended up watching Netflix most days. First, it was just one show during lunch. But then, it was hard to get off the sofa. She started drinking a glass of wine while watching her shows. She told me she just wasn't motivated. Her husband was mad because she didn't get anything done.

The underlying truth was Sheila felt lost. Her daughter, who had been so dependent, no longer needed her. Sheila even missed the drama. The movies and wine numbed her pain. As we dug deeper, Shelia realized she'd stayed on that couch because she was waiting for her daughter to call; basically, she was waiting for her purpose to return.

Newsflash, Mom. Purpose isn't going to suddenly show up while you're eating chips and guac on your sofa watching reruns of *Gilmore*

*Girls*. When we're too comfortable, we're not tapping into ESSENCE and we're not growing. Just like plants, if we're not growing, we start to wither and die; we put ourselves at risk for depression and despair.

Discomfort makes us move. It pushes us off the couch and makes us grow. Humans need novelty to thrive. It boosts serotonin and dopamine, those feel-good body chemicals.

So, if you feel stuck on the couch or anywhere, ask yourself what will entice you to move. If you're thinking, *I'm never on the couch; I'm busy from morning until night and always on the move*, be careful here, your busyness may very well be your comfort zone—keeping you stuck in a routine that doesn't allow for novelty or growth. In that case, ask yourself: What will make me happy and proud of myself?

You can be busy and still be avoiding the uncomfortable things that will dial up your dream. Goodness knows, I'm guilty of this. It's amazing what seems like fun when you're avoiding writing a book (cleaning out the refrigerator or vacuuming the lint off the back of the dryer).

Truly, the greatest joys in life are always on the other side of our comfort zone. I hate discomfort as much as anyone else, but life is rigged this way. We have to push through the discomfort to get to the growth and joy.

## Turning Your Dial Up

As we've seen, it takes courage to dial up your dream. In Brené Brown's *The Gifts of Imperfection*, she reminds us that the Latin root of the word courage is *cor*, which means heart. Courage comes through the heart. Your mind is often the skeptic and will give you one million reasons why you should stay where you are. But when you start to face your fears, resolve to do the uncomfortable thing, choose to hope again, and raise your expectations for your life, something that's bigger than you and stronger than any resistance starts stirring in your heart.

Courage is the energy behind action. Now that you're developing yours, use it as you take the following steps to dialing up your dream.

## Step 1: Make a Commitment to Yourself

Write out a one-sentence commitment to yourself. It can be as simple as, "I commit to get off the couch and do one thing every day that makes my surroundings more pleasant." Or, "I will go online and look at the classes offered by the community college."

There is power in commitment—and now that power is yours.

## Step 2: Assess Where You Are

In order to know where you want to go, you must first understand where you are. So, pull out your exercises and notes from your first draft of your Mom Story, your second draft, and the work you did in the previous chapter. Identify where you may have lost hope or given up on something you wanted. Think about how you might now be in a position to go for it. Sit with this. Then journal. Think about using your courage to reach for the dial, hope again, and tell yourself that what you want is possible. This practice is key to having a joy-filled future.

## Step 3: Invest in You

Investing in ourselves can be especially hard for moms; we're used to investing in our daughters, after all. But now it's your turn. You're worth it. Invest in a workshop, training session, or class that will bring you closer to your dream or that you would simply enjoy. Though it may feel selfish, investing in yourself really is selfless. The more you live to your full potential, the more everyone in your life benefits. You'll be happier and fulfilled versus resentful, irritable, and needy.

## Step 4: Get Support

As your daughter inched closer to her dreams, you were there as her biggest cheerleader. You helped her stay on task. You brought in other professionals when needed to help her get clear about her future. There have been coaches, counselors, college advisors, teachers, and youth ministers. There was—and probably still is—a whole team to help her dial up her dream.

Do this for yourself. You are more likely to get where you want to go with support. I know for a fact that I couldn't have moved the needle one bit toward my dream without a coach. All along the way, I needed mentors who knew more than I did, who could point me in the right direction. I also needed accountability, which has come from my peers and not my family. When I told my mom I was writing my first book, she said, "Why?" She thought it was the craziest thing she'd ever heard. After I published *Dial Down the Drama*, she bragged about it to all her friends.

Ask yourself what kind of support you need and who can best give it. Consider hiring a housekeeper or someone to run errands. If you want to start an organizing business, do you know any organizers you could invite to lunch? Consider that a therapist might help you process any obstacles in your path and cheer you on as you move closer to your dream.

## Step 5: Write Out Your Goals

Look at what it is you want and break it up into clear, practical, and doable goals. Remember, a clear goal is specific and measurable. "I want to work out," is not a clear goal. "I am going to do an hour workout at the gym on Monday, Wednesday, and Friday at 8 a.m.," is.

Research has shown that the simple act of writing down your goals increases the probability of you reaching them considerably. That probability increases even further when you have a coach or an accountability partner.

There are two kinds of goals: process goals and end goals. Your process goals assist you in getting to your end goal. For example, a process goal is: "I will write one hour a day, Monday through Friday, at 9 a.m." An end goal is: "I will have a finished manuscript by June 11." The process goal of writing an hour a day leads to you to finish your manuscript and achieve your end goal.

You don't need a coach or an accountability buddy to write a goal. You can start now. What is one goal for yourself? It can be a process or an end goal. (Hint: Process goals are the easiest way to start.) Now, write it down and go reach it.

## Step 6: Take Action

While commitment, support, training, and goals are important, you have to take action to turn the dial and move toward your dream. This week, commit to your goal—and do it. If it's helpful, reach out to a friend and tell them what you plan, then report back to them when you've taken action.

## Living Your Dream

Right now, you're standing in front of the door of the Play Big Zone. What do you want? Do you want to be like half the people in my mastermind group, who didn't do anything? Or do you want to be that person who, with the right support, is creating miracles? That's the choice we get to make every day. What do you choose?

By the time your daughter is in her mid-twenties, she'll likely have a new set of friends and will have expanded her connections. She'll have had new experiences that developed her gifts and abilities. She'll have matured and become more responsible from being on her own. Despite all the doubt, the struggle, and the difficulties, dialing up her dream will have been totally worth it.

And you will be in this new phase too—where changing your life for the better means having the courage to make different decisions. I'm inviting you to step through the door. I'm inviting you to dial up your dream.

## Exercise: One Click Closer

THIS EXERCISE helps you to explore what deliberately turning the dial feels like for you. It doesn't have to be a big turn. One small click toward becoming more yourself will do.

1   Think of something you loved to do that you gave up on when you were busy parenting.

2   Do it.

Here are some ideas to consider:

- get tickets for a concert and invite a friend;
- attend a reading at your local bookstore;
- learn to sea kayak;
- sign up to usher at your community theater (or, better yet, try out for their next show);
- do a bike trail with a friend;
- take a memoir class online or join a writer's group;
- find a noncredit course of interest and take it.

3   After you do whatever you choose, open up your journal and record how you felt as you signed up, as you showed up, and after you did it.

4   The next time you talk to your daughter, tell her about your adventure. Note how you felt telling her about it as well as her reaction.

5   Repeat the first four steps until you are living your dream!

## 12

# The Choice

I T WAS EARLY. I was barely awake as I stumbled through the clinic door to get my annual mammogram. Betty, the technician, led me into the room. She was annoyingly chatty for 6 a.m. As she was trying to squeeze one of my girls between two cold metal plates, she asked me what I did for a living. I said, "I'm a therapist. I help moms have good relationships with their teens."

Betty asked if I'd written a book. I told her I had. Then she told me, "Don't move." As she took the picture, she said, "I won't read it. I don't read self-help books." Then she grabbed my other girl and mashed it down on a cold metal plate and continued, "I used to love watching my daughter sleep." When I asked her why, she replied, "Because when she was awake, she was a fire-breathing dragon."

I laughed. What else could I do? This whole situation was so absurd.

As she was setting me up for the last picture and turned that last crank of the compression paddle (the one that makes it so you practically can't breathe), she said, "You know, I prayed a Mother Curse on her."

*What the...?!* My girl flat as a pancake from that last crank, my face smashed into the mammogram machine, I barely squeaked out, "What's a Mother Curse?"

"Don't move," she said. Then added, "I pray she has a daughter who will be as mean to her as she was to me."

*Really?*

She released the machine. Thank God I was free. I walked out thinking, *How sad.*

## Steer Clear of the Mother Curse

Betty's defenses were impenetrable; she wasn't open to knowing another way. Her mom probably prayed the Mother Curse on her, and now she is passing it to the next generation.

My guess is that Betty's prayer is not your prayer, or you wouldn't be reading the last chapter of this book. We don't want to be cursing the next generation; we want to be blessing them. This is why I do what I do. I want to change these generational patterns for good. I want mothers and daughters to bring out the best in each other, not the worst.

Unfortunately, this Mother Curse is a thing. I was talking to a group of moms, and I asked them if they knew about the Mother Curse. They all did. In fact, they recited it together. Scary.

Sure, the mother-daughter relationship is filled with challenges, especially in the teen and emerging-adult years. But now you know, Mom, that so much of the drama can be managed, that you get to decide how to approach each interaction with your daughter, and you get to choose the type of relationship you want to develop between you.

When the hard times come (the grinding wheel), now you know you can use them to help you and your daughter grow as individuals while deepening your understanding of each other. Or, like Betty, you can see them as payback time—a chance for your child to experience some of the hell you've suffered and a chance for you to revert into a twelve-year-old mean-girl mindset. You can decide.

Day by day, decision by decision, you're laying the foundation of your mother-daughter relationship for years to come, and maybe even for her relationship with her own daughter someday. With the insights, self-awareness, and tools you've found in this book, you have what you need to create a mother-daughter relationship that's a blessing to both of you.

Now, the only task left is to set your intention for exactly what you'd like that relationship to be. This is not about micromanaging or getting your daughter to carry out your dreams for her; not, "I want my daughter to marry the right man" or "I want my daughter to get a high-powered job." No. This is about you deciding on your aims for your relationship with your young adult daughter so you know better how to achieve them.

Here are some things that I want for my relationship with my daughter:

- I want to stay connected and current with her.

- I want her to know I'll be there when she needs me and I'm available to help.

- I want her to feel free to live her own life.

- I want to give her the space to reinvent herself.

- I want to continue to be friend-like and have positive experiences together.

- I want to be there to celebrate her when there are significant markers in her life.

- I want her to know I believe in her and couldn't be prouder of her.

- I want to enjoy her and our time together.

- I want to be a significant part of her family.

- I want to be a positive model of adulthood and continue growing and living my dreams.

- I want us to be able to do difficult things together and turn our hard conversations into meaningful conversations.

- I want to allow for the new and not dredge up the past.

- And I never, ever want my daughter to feel pressured, obligated, manipulated, judged, burdened, or forced into a relationship with me.

These are my intentions. This doesn't mean I always act in a way that's supportive of each one—I don't, and I won't. I still get bossy and sometimes slip into self-pity. And I'm pretty sure I will continue to do so from time to time. When I do go astray, however, I need only look to my intentions and use them as guideposts to steer me back to having the relationship with my daughter I really want. Such intentionality keeps us strong and on target when things get shaky.

Now it's your turn. What are your intentions for your relationship with your daughter today? In five, ten, or twenty years? What do you want your relationship to look like and feel like to both of you? What do you want for your relationship when your daughter is fully grounded in life with a career, perhaps a marriage or children? Who will you be to each other—when life goes well and when it doesn't work out the way either of you would have wanted? I encourage you to take thirty minutes here and record your intentions in your journal.

Getting clear on what you want that future to be allows you to use each interaction to support your intention. It helps you to steer clear of the Mother Curse so you can foster a relationship that's a blessing— one that will enrich both your lives with enough wisdom, love, and joy that it can't help but spill into the next generation and the next.

## The Mothering Urge

For all our efforts in setting intentions and being purposeful as we move toward a more mature mother-daughter relationship, one thing that can (and will) knock us off course on occasion is falling prey to the Mothering Urge—the urge to control our daughters, to offer them unsolicited advice, to "fix" their problems, and to take the slightest slight by them personally.

Almost instinctive by now, these urges don't go away when our daughters turn twenty-one, thirty, or sixty-five. Though the majority of these impulses may have had their place in our earlier parenting, with some even proving beneficial, they can now be quite destructive as our daughters work toward establishing themselves as adults.

My client Whitney, a financial analyst, is forty-eight years old and has two girls in college. She's been divorced for five years and is thriving. While Whitney was remodeling her home recently, her mother, Martha, came over unannounced almost daily to criticize Whitney's choices. She commented negatively on Whitney's paint selections. She disliked the kitchen countertops. And when the couch Whitney ordered was delivered, Martha shrieked, "You got a white sofa? For heaven's sake, what a big mistake."

These criticisms were no surprise to Whitney. All through her adulthood, her mother has offered unwanted advice. "Why would you wear (fill in the blank) to (fill in the blank)?" is a regular refrain from Martha. Worse, Whitney knows that when she ignores such comments, her mother takes it as a personal affront—as if Whitney chooses her outfits or her furniture with the purpose of upsetting her mother. Still, the constant criticism is painful, and frankly, Whitney regards it as one more thing to deal with in her already busy life. So, throughout her adult life, Whitney has avoided being with her mother as much as possible.

Once your daughter is an adult, her choices are no longer your business—especially if the situation is not a life-threatening one. This doesn't mean that your opinion or thinking isn't right or wise. And you may have the urge to speak up when you feel she's headed down the wrong path—like when she announces she's getting a puppy and you know she travels every week for work, or she tells you her boyfriend cheated on her for the tenth time but she won't leave him, or she decides to get a gigantic tattoo on her arm right before a big interview with an accounting firm. (You know I could go on.)

But, Mom, realize this: Whatever you say isn't going to change anything. In fact, her feeling your disapproval only makes things worse between you and shuts down the communication. If you must say something, limit it to: "Are you sure that's what you want?" When she says yes, accept it. Because it will be her decision and her life now.

Also, when you feel that urge to give unsolicited advice, you might ask yourself why. Do you really think your daughter is incapable of figuring things out for herself? (I dare say, that's how Martha justified her interference in Whitney's life.) But if you dig a little deeper and turn that lens back on yourself, you might find you interfere because you're afraid of no longer being needed, of becoming irrelevant to your daughter's life, of having no relationship with her at all (likely closer to Martha's truth).

Even if being irrelevant were a possibility—and it's not—you can't arm wrestle, criticize, or guilt your daughter into a relationship. You can't force your daughter to have a relationship with you. The Mothering Urge can stem from your need to be needed. But your daughter's job is not to meet your needs. Meeting your needs is your job.

The paradox is when you let go of these Mothering Urges, your daughter voluntarily comes to you. You attract bees with honey. Don't be a fly swatter.

There are and will continue to be times you'll have the urge to swaddle your daughter in bubble wrap, treating her as if she were a child to keep her from the harm and cruelty of the world. What you really want, though—what many of these urges are about—is to have certainty for her and for you. You want to know that things are okay now and that they're going to stay that way. That she's on the right track and her entire future is going to work out.

As mothers, we want to believe that we can control our children's future. Of course, this is absurd. As if we have any control over what happens to us in the next minute or two—let alone our daughters over a lifetime.

The antidote for the Mothering Urge is to tap into something more solid and strong inside of you—trust. This isn't a hope-that-it-is-true trust. This is a gritty trust built from two decades of mothering and connection with your daughter. You trust the mother you've been and the daughter you have. You trust that you have laid the foundation and groundwork for your daughter—all the things that you taught her as a child. You trust all the ways you have spoken into her life. All the ways you have supported her and lifted her up when she was fragile, heartbroken, and lost. With every talk, every hug, every loving act, you planted all your knowledge and strength inside her.

So, now you can rest knowing that you are with her even when she is away from you. You have taught her to know the truth of who she is. Trust that she will follow it. Fear and doubt will pound on your door. But trust in who your daughter is and that she can find her way through any situation. She will have her own grinding wheels, and this is good. It will make her a more beautiful human. Love her, pray, hold space for her, and know your connection is enough.

I'm not saying any of this is easy. The Mothering Urge is not a gentle whisper. It is a mighty force of nature swirling around our brains like a hurricane. But when we know our urges and patterns and what triggers them, we can resist acting on them—or at least, we can work on that.

Our daughters have a right to their own lives. We have a right to retire our monitor and enjoy our new role as consultant. A relationship that's a blessing supports this evolution.

## Be Flexible

Part of being in any relationship is the willingness to bend—sometimes more than you think you should have to. This can be harder in a relationship where you have had the upper hand for a couple of decades, where your daughter, as the child, has been expected to bend to your benevolent will. But she is not your little girl anymore. Because you've parented her well, she is soon to become her own woman.

As your daughter settles into a career and perhaps settles down with a partner, you're likely to have more flexibility in your schedule than she will. Remember that. Be respectful of where she is in life when you make plans, ask a favor, or ask for her time—and be flexible.

One of my clients, Liana, is married and has two small children. Every summer, she struggles with her in-laws over the family vacation. Her in-laws own a second home in Wyoming. All the grown kids and grandchildren are expected to spend two full weeks there together. There's no flexibility in the scheduling—no coming for one week or an extended weekend.

This is a grown-up version of forced family fun. Liana is absolutely miserable the whole two weeks. She resents that it takes up all her and her husband's vacation time every year. Her husband hates it, too, but feels like he can't cross his mother.

Yet, the mother-in-law sees her invitation as generous—a gift, even. In her mind, she's ensuring her grown children and their families have time together to create shared memories and strengthen bonds. She's not wrong. Hosting such an occasion is wonderful. But her being so rigid about the two weeks and not considering that these working adults only get so much vacation a year makes this "gift" mighty costly for the families involved. Everyone may be sitting around the fireplace together, but no one wants to be there. She's lost their hearts and lost the joy.

Healthy relationships make room for flexibility. My personal experience is that when I loosen my death grip on my plans, something even better usually comes of it.

I love to be in control. I love having my plans nailed down. Raising a child, however, quickly taught me that my freakish control mode wasn't realistic, certainly not when it came to another human being, and particularly not when that other human being was my free-spirited yet headstrong daughter. In our eighteen years under the same roof, she kindly drove that message home to me a million times over in a million different ways.

To this day, any plans I make with my daughter shape-shift. I know this. So, my choice comes down to clinging to my need for control or not making plans with her at all. Of course, I choose to make plans, knowing this will require me to be flexible, to go with her flow.

For instance, when my daughter first moved to California, she canceled our annual trip to Colorado that we'd been taking since she was a small child. I was hugely disappointed. But later that summer, she suggested I meet her in Big Sur and Carmel. That trip turned out be a totally wonderful adventure for both of us. More important, though, because we were not in our traditional vacation place, we didn't fall into our usual mother-daughter patterns. The California coast presented an unexpected opportunity to explore a new way of being together and to lay some groundwork for our adult mother-daughter relationship.

When we are flexible, we are more likely to see things as they are. So, we address what is—the real circumstances—instead of being stuck in what we wish were true. Even our best-laid plans will lead us to roadblocks, detours, and big disappointments in life.

When a daughter veers from "the plan," it can take a toll on a mother's heart. While we need to honor those feelings and grieve what's lost, we also need to remind ourselves to be flexible and look to what can be. Think of all the times your life has veered from the straight and narrow. Remember how your own mother may have had to go with your flow—and maybe your daughter did too.

Cultivating flexibility allows us to see hurdles as fodder for novel solutions. Despite how bad they can feel in the moment, when we confront them and are flexible, they strengthen us and lead us to a better road we didn't even know was there.

## When in Doubt, Choose Love

One of the hardest things I've ever worked on is my TEDx talk. *Dial Down the Drama* had just been published, and this talk would summarize the book. Like everyone else, I had a limited time onstage. Meaning I had to boil down close to three hundred pages into twelve minutes—a daunting task. Every word in the talk was precious real estate. After six months of wrestling with what really mattered in all those pages, what the book was really saying to moms with newly minted teenage daughters, it came to me: *Choose love over judgment.*

As your teenager transitions into adulthood, those words only become more critical. Unfortunately, judgment comes too naturally to us. Your daughter will make life choices that grind against your values and preferences—you can count on that. In our fear, we jump to judgment, hoping our negative attitude will be persuasive and will bring her back to the good sense she was raised to have.

As surprising and perhaps upsetting as some of your daughter's choices are going to be, being judgmental isn't going to help you here, and it certainly won't help your daughter. Your judgment slaps a label on her as flawed, other, or broken. The label blocks you from seeing the beautiful human being she is. It also makes her feel misunderstood and unloved by the person she needs most to support her as she takes risks, tries new things, and stretches to find who she is and who she's going to become.

Judgment attacks our core essence and says we are not worthy of love and belonging. As Brené Brown writes so powerfully in *The Gifts of Imperfection*, "Worthy now. Not if. Not when. We are worthy of love and belonging *now*. Right this minute." Judgment builds walls and blinds both of you to this expansive potential of connection that you can discover throughout your lifetime.

Thankfully, judgment is never a foregone conclusion. You always have a choice. You can always choose love.

Just last week my daughter assisted me in choosing love. She called knowing I had laryngitis. When I answered the phone, she said, "Mom, I just want you to listen." She went on about how her business was growing and her schedule was full of private clients. She was so excited, but she also expressed concern at being a little overwhelmed with managing everything. I didn't say a word . . . because I couldn't.

As the call was winding down, she said, "Thanks, Mom, for listening to me. This helped so much. I knew if I could just say things out loud, I could figure them out." And then she laughed. "Okay, I'm going to tell you this one last thing and it's a good thing you have laryngitis. I just got another tattoo of a bee on my arm." She was right, it was a good thing I had laryngitis.

As moms of adults, our job now is to listen more and talk less (maybe it always was). We may disagree with our daughters. And that's okay. We are people with opinions too. But when we choose to respond with love, not judgment, our point of view is more likely to be sought and considered. When you choose love over judgment, you always come down on the right side for a strong relationship.

Keep your heart open to your daughter. Love is what heals. Love is what motivates. Love is what will last when our time on earth comes to an end.

## The Blessing of My Mom

While I was in high school, my mom and I definitely struggled. I'm sure I gave her more than a few gray hairs. When I was away at college, things were better between us. I think for my mom—as with most of us—the old adage "out of sight, out of mind" came into play.

When I moved home for my last semester before graduation, the tensions came right back. I don't remember too many details—which is probably a good thing. I'm not even sure why I irritated her so much. At twenty-one, I was pretty oblivious to my self-absorption and my mom's feelings. What I do remember is she was frustrated with me all the time.

It got to the point where one day she looked me right in the eye and said, "One of us is going to have to leave this house, and it's not me." I was stunned by this proclamation, stunned that my mom would even hint at evicting me—*me*—from my childhood home (which speaks to the high level of security I had in her love for me). Luckily, I would only be under her roof—and feet—a few more weeks. Then I'd be off to my summer job in Colorado and, in the fall, graduate school in Arkansas.

When I returned to Houston after graduate school, my mom's mom, whom I called Nana, was dying of lung cancer. Nana was my rock, my anchor, and my encourager. She loved me to the moon and back even in my turbulent teens. Losing Nana was devastating for both my mom and me. Living through Nana's passing together, leaning on each other, cleansed decades of resentment and anger between my mom and me—and we became close again.

Or at least that's the story I told myself at the time. What I can see now, however, is that my relationship with my mother changed because I'd changed. I'd grown up in those three years in Arkansas, and my mother had given me the space—and security—to do it. Thus, I returned to Houston mature enough to rise to the occasion, to be there for Nana, and to be there fully for my mother, though I was grieving too.

Turns out my mother was excellent at ushering me through my "adulting." She always kept a warm home base for me but never made me feel like I was tied to it. My mom had a life. She had a good relationship with my father. She volunteered in the community. My parents had a big group of friends with whom they went to dinner and the theater, and often traveled. She had her own friends as well, with whom she played golf, took art history classes, attended a book club, and played cards.

My mom's active life not only set a good example for me, it also kept me from worrying about her. She was the opposite of needy. She wasn't trying to live her life through me. She didn't pry. She let me figure my life out. I know she wasn't thrilled when I, her daughter with a master's degree, took a full-time position not in my field that barely paid me enough to get by. But she kept that (and so much more) to herself.

Because my mom didn't pressure me or try to control me, I wanted to talk to her. I sought her advice. I was usually the one who called, and she'd follow my lead. Which made me want to hang out with her more.

Starting in my mid-twenties, I went to my parents' house for Sunday dinners—and I honestly regarded it as a highlight of my week. My mom would prepare a wonderful meal and set the table with tablecloth and crystal wine glasses. I would relax. I felt pampered and loved. Those Sunday dinners acted as a stable support as I continued to grow my adult legs.

As time went on, my mom and I became more friend-like. We were good shopping buddies with similar tastes. We both love art, and so on a regular basis we'd have lunch and go see the latest exhibit at a local museum or gallery.

As I've said, my marriage wasn't the best. After I gave birth to my daughter, my husband at the time wasn't helpful. But my mom was. She took care of me and my daughter. Often my husband was rude to her, but she never reacted to him. She stayed clear in her intention to be supportive of me. She resisted the urge to tell us fumbling young parents what to do or point out the issues in my marriage. Now, I can see how much willpower that took.

My mom was by my side for the entire first month of my daughter's life. Right after that, on a cruise with my dad and some friends,

Mom collapsed. She ended up in an emergency room in Puerto Rico, comatose and unresponsive. I remember getting the phone call, holding my four-week-old baby and praying my mom wouldn't die.

She'd had a heart attack. They flew her home. When I finally saw her, I was in shock. She was still unresponsive. She had a blank stare, like she was a million miles away. She'd lost oxygen to her brain during the incident. We didn't know how much of her would come back. I remember her looking at my infant daughter and my dad saying, "You need to get better. You don't want to miss seeing your granddaughter grow up." And somehow, Mom rallied. It was a miracle. I witnessed a determination deep inside of her that inspires me to this day.

As my daughter grew, my mom became a favored playmate. She championed pretend play (I'd rather watch paint dry). She and my daughter would play puppy doctor for hours, healing all the stuffed animals. She played every pretend princess story in existence. When my daughter insisted that she wear the princess dress and my mom be the witch—which was every time they played—my mom would always push back and squabble with her over it.

When I got divorced, my mom was there one hundred percent for me. She forwent the judgment and instead chose to steady me with her strength, approval, and unwavering confidence in me as I rebuilt my life.

Today, my mom is eighty-nine years old. My dad passed three years ago. She's in the last stages of dementia. I've been able to keep her in her home with round-the-clock care. I still go to her house every Sunday, though things are different. She no longer makes me a home-cooked meal, but we do regularly get a flatbread California club pizza (her favorite) and enjoy it together. When the weather is nice, we sit on the back porch and look out onto the golf course. I bring my dog, Lilly, over. Despite being fifty-five pounds and half pit bull and half blue heeler, Lilly is gentle and nurturing to Mom.

Though my mom often gets confused about my name now, she knows who I am. It's hard to have a conversation. But I've discovered being with her is enough. In these last few years, she's taught me more about presence and mindfulness than any guru could. We listen to the birds and to the wind rustle through the trees. We watch Lilly roll around in the grass. We watch the cardinals, wrens, woodpeckers, and mockingbirds visit the birdfeeders. We notice that the roses, azaleas, and daffodils are blooming.

We sit in silence with a lifetime of hard and cherished memories between us. When all the words finally leave, there will be love and that love between us will never die.

## Your Life, Your Dream, Your Choice

Now I'm the one with the young adult daughter. The many gifts my mom passed to me through our relationship, I want to give my daughter. I never felt burdened by my mom. My mom respected my freedom. My mom continued to dial up her dream and work on her physical, intellectual, social, and spiritual life my entire life, which showed me the importance of living fully. I will do the same for my daughter. I know it took incredible discipline and restraint for my perfectionist mother not to tell me how to live my life and raise my baby. Because she did it, I know I can.

Mom, you are a daughter too. Think about your own adult relationship with your mother. What has it been like? What did you appreciate? How did those good things affect you? Where did the Mothering Urge overtake her at times? How did that feel to you? How did it change your behavior toward her? What aspects of your relationship with your mother do you want to bring to your relationship with your daughter and which do you want to leave behind?

When you embrace the blessing of your emerging-adult daughter, you open the door to healing, to life, to love, and to a delicious feast. There will be trials and suffering ahead for her and for you. There will be disagreements between you. But when you build a relationship founded in love, that relationship will stand strong.

You are the mom. You determine this next phase of your life with your daughter. It's within your power to lead the way and make room for you both to dial up your dreams. To be adults. To become each other's biggest cheerleaders and strongest supports throughout your lives. To create a legacy of blessings between mother and daughter for generations to come.

What greater gift could a mother ask for or give? The choice is yours.

When all is said and done, the sharp words, the hurt, the drama will fade over time like an old scar. What's left is a deep gratitude. Not just for the happy times but for the whole difficult, dangerous, and delightful journey you and your daughter have traveled. And when you get there, I know you wouldn't trade it for the world.

# Acknowledgments

---

**I** AM SO GRATEFUL...

I wrote this book for all of you dear moms who have shared your heart, your confusion, frustration, joy, and sadness as your daughter made her jagged journey to adulthood. I have listened to you—my community of moms in my office, on Zoom, in my programs, in my audience—and I saw a need. I wanted to honor your voices, your hearts, and your experiences. When I asked you questions on social media, you were there and shared your stories and once again confirmed why this book is needed. I wrote this book so that you'd know you're not alone. I wanted to help you avoid the common pitfalls and guide you in this ambiguous time.

I'm grateful for Steve Harrison. During our coaching day we riffed on titles and came up with *Dial Up the Dream*. You helped me see this book's tremendous value for moms and daughters.

Thank you, Christine Kane, for challenging me once again. After sharing with you that my book concept had just been shot down by someone influential (which caused me to stall out for nine months), you simply said, "Why don't you just *write the book*." You directed me back to my own power. At that moment I *knew* I was supposed to write *Dial Up the Dream*.

Beth Brand, you made writing this book fun and enjoyable. You are an amazing book coach and were able to corral my wild herd of ideas and make them flow. You got my message and me up close and personal since you've "been there and done that" with your own son. This created a great synergy.

Since this was my second book, I decided to make the writing process more enjoyable. You've heard of destination weddings; well, I had destination chapters.

I am grateful for the incredible beauty of La Jolla, California, where I wrote Chapter 3 and the introduction. Thank you to the Grande Colonial Hotel for upgrading me to a suite with a lovely view of the Pacific Ocean (yes, I was inspired) when you found out I was writing a book.

Thank you again, Christine Kane, for gifting me your beautiful Airbnb in the mountains of Asheville, North Carolina. Though I hadn't intended this, it provided amazing synchronicity as I wrote Chapter 11. I traveled to Asheville numerous times for Uplevel You retreats. They were instrumental in dialing up *my* dream.

Thank you, Steve and Sherry Duson, for your generosity and letting me stay in your cozy casita in Tucson, Arizona. Again, it was perfect synchronicity. I was working on Chapter 10 and didn't know how to start it. But after returning from our hike through the Saguaro National Park, all the pieces came together, and you were kind enough to share your story, which I know will inspire many.

Thank you, Elizabeth Barbour, for quickly pulling together a writing retreat and inviting Whitney, Sara, Lianna, and me to your family farm near Pinehurst, North Carolina. Sitting on the front porch, staring at the tall pine trees, was a perfect way to write the last chapter. It was so fun to work, enjoy happy hour by the lake, and share my writing with such encouraging women.

I am thankful for my Airbnb on a big Texas ranch in the hill country in Bandera. This is where I wrote Chapters 4 and 7. I wrote these in the throes of Covid, so I was safely quarantining with deer, turkeys, foxes, coyotes, armadillos, and a host of stars, which kept me entertained and inspired.

There is no way I would have written this book without great accountability.

Thank you, Sue Ludwig, for being an amazing friend and accountability buddy. What a gift that we went through this writing process together and could cheer each other on as we both wrote and had to *live* our individual books. It was so helpful to know that when I was writing on Saturday, you were too.

Elaine Bailey, thank you for being your cheery, brilliant self and for being there for me every week on our accountability calls.

I'm grateful for my Houston homies, Ann, Joan, and Rochelle, and our mastermind group. Every month sitting in Ann's beautiful backyard, I enjoyed a glass of wine and great conversation. Y'all cheered me on and helped me get through Covid.

And I'm thankful for my many friends who've walked this process and shared their ideas, stories, and encouragement: Julia, Kia, Tom, Lorna, Jennifer, Erika, and Jenny.

I'm grateful for Jesse Finkelstein for both her enthusiasm over *Dial Up the Dream* and for graciously welcoming me to the wonderful team (Rony, Lorraine, Emily) at Page Two.

And saving the best for last...

I am extremely grateful for my sister, Cathy Harris, who has been one of my biggest cheerleaders since the day I was born. She is always there for me and prayerfully has my back.

I am thankful for my mom, who modeled how to be a marvelous mother to an adult daughter. And now I know how hard that can be.

And to my cherished daughter, I love you to the moon and back. I am grateful to witness the unfolding of your unique shiny self. I admire your convictions, your strength, your creativity, your beauty inside and out, your zest for living, and your fire. (Though I haven't always been grateful for your fire!) I am most appreciative for how you challenge me to not settle and to be a better human being.

ANGI LEWIS PHOTOGRAPHY

# About the Author

COLLEEN O'GRADY, MA, is a licensed therapist, coach, and trainer who helps moms reduce drama, reclaim their lives, and dial up their dreams with their teen and young adult daughters. After fifty thousand hours of working with moms and daughters and having lived it with her own daughter, she published her award-winning and bestselling book *Dial Down the Drama: Reducing Conflict and Reconnecting with Your Teenage Daughter—A Guide for Mothers Everywhere.*

Colleen has shared her message of practical hope with moms worldwide in *Parents* magazine, *Wall Street Journal Lunch Break*, popular parenting podcasts, and on the red carpet at TEDxWilmington. Colleen is the host of the *Power Your Parenting: Moms with Teens* podcast; in 2021, it was ranked number one among podcasts on parenting teens.

Learn more about Colleen at colleenogrady.com, and connect with her on Facebook, Instagram, LinkedIn, and Twitter.